Helping Clients Deal with Adversity by Changing Their Attitudes

Helping Clients Deal with Adversity by Changing Their Attitudes: A Concise Therapist Guide provides an outline for therapists wishing to help clients deal with life's adversities by encouraging them to change their attitudes.

Divided in two parts, this book first provides a thorough, but concise, introduction to an attitude-based approach to therapy, then applies these ideas to therapy. By redefining established concepts of 'rational' and 'irrational' beliefs in terms of the 'rigidity' and 'extremity' of client attitudes, Professor Dryden puts forward a language and an approach that is more acceptable to both clients and therapists.

Helping Clients Deal with Adversity by Changing Their Attitudes will be a great asset to clinical and counselling psychologists, counsellors, and psychotherapists as well as trainees in these areas. It will be particularly of interest to CBT practitioners and students who do not cover REBT in their training but are looking for a concise guide to how its attitudinal focus can be understood and applied in clinical practice.

Windy Dryden is in clinical and consultative practice and is an international authority on Cognitive Behaviour Therapy. He is Emeritus Professor of Psychotherapeutic Studies at Goldsmiths, University of London. He has worked in psychotherapy for more than 40 years and is the author or editor of over 230 books.

Routledge Focus on Mental Health

Routledge Focus on Mental Health presents short books on current topics, linking in with cutting-edge research and practice.

For a full list of titles in this series, please visit www.routledge.com/Routledge-Focus-on-Mental-Health/book-series/RFMH

Titles in the series:

Helping Clients Deal with Adversity by Changing their Attitudes
A Concise Therapist Guide
Windy Dryden

Single-Session 'One-at-a-Time' Therapy
A Rational Emotive Behaviour Therapy Approach
Windy Dryden

Working with Interpreters in Psychological Therapy
The Right to be Understood
Jude Boyles and Nathalie Talbot

Rational Emotive Behaviour Therapy
A Newcomer's Guide
Walter J. Matweychuk and Windy Dryden

The Feldenkrais Method for Executive Coaches, Managers, and Business Leaders
Moving in All Directions
Paul Ogden and Garet Newell

An Evidence-based Approach to Authentic Leadership Development
Tony Fusco

Helping Clients Deal with Adversity by Changing Their Attitudes

A Concise Therapist Guide

Windy Dryden

Routledge
Taylor & Francis Group
LONDON AND NEW YORK

First published 2019
by Routledge
2 Park Square, Milton Park, Abingdon, Oxon OX14 4RN

and by Routledge
52 Vanderbilt Avenue, New York, NY 10017

Routledge is an imprint of the Taylor & Francis Group, an informa business

British Library Cataloguing-in-Publication Data
A catalogue record for this book is available from the British Library

Library of Congress Cataloging-in-Publication Data
A catalog record has been requested for this book

ISBN: 978-0-367-27563-1 (hbk)
ISBN: 978-0-429-29664-2 (ebk)

Typeset in Times New Roman
by Newgen Publishing UK

Contents

Introduction

In this book, I present a concise guide for therapists wishing to help clients deal with life's adversities by encouraging them to change their rigid and extreme attitudes towards these adversities to more functional, flexible and non-extreme attitudes. The book is based on the theory and practice of Rational Emotive Behaviour Therapy (REBT). In that theory, these two sets of attitudes were previously known as irrational beliefs and rational beliefs respectively. In this guide I put forward language that, I believe, is more acceptable to both clients and therapists (see also Dryden, 2016). My major goal is to make an attitude-based approach to therapy more accessible to therapists and to do so in a concise manner.

The guide is divided into two parts. In Part 1, entitled 'The role of attitudes in psychological disturbance and health in the face of adversity', I explain my use of the term 'attitudes' rather than the term 'beliefs' and present a careful delineation of rigid and extreme attitudes towards adversity and the pivotal role that these attitudes play in psychological disturbance in the face of adversity. Then, I present a careful delineation of flexible and non-extreme attitudes towards the same adversity and the central role that these attitudes play in a psychologically healthy response to the adversity. Another aspect covered in Part 1 is the importance of focusing on what the client finds particularly troubling in the situation in which they have a problem. This is known as the adversity and I show how even in a clear-cut situation, such as failing to be promoted, a client can disturb themself about different aspects of this situation (Dryden, 2018). In doing so, I demonstrate my points with a client case that runs through the book.

Another feature of Part 1 is that I show in a concise way how rigid and extreme attitudes interact with adversities to lead to a variety of disturbed emotional, behavioural and thinking consequences and how, by contrast, flexible and non-extreme attitudes lead to a variety of healthy emotional, behavioural and thinking consequences (Dryden, 2016).

Part 2, entitled 'Helping clients change their attitudes towards adversity', I deal with the application of the ideas discussed in Part 1 to the arena of individual therapy. In doing so, I cover some of the main ways that a therapist can encourage their client to stand back and examine their attitudes in a manner that helps them to commit themself to choose to develop flexible and non-extreme attitudes. I then cover a number of ways that the therapist can assist the client in developing such attitudes.

I also provide a number of appendices for reference purposes as well as a list for suggested further reading.

Windy Dryden
London and Eastbourne
January 2019

Part 1

The role of attitudes in psychological disturbance and health in the face of adversity

In this part of the book, I discuss the role of attitudes in psychological disturbance and health in the face of adversity. In particular, I distinguish between rigid and flexible attitudes and discuss the extreme and non-extreme attitudes that are derived from each respectively.

Using a case study, I detail the emotive, behavioural and cognitive consequences of rigid/extreme attitudes and flexible/non-extreme attitudes and show how the former are the hallmark of disturbed responses to adversities and the latter are the hallmark of healthy responses to the same adversities.

Introduction

An inherent feature of human beings is our tendency to like certain things and dislike others. Most of us like similar things in life (e.g. being approved and doing well at things that are important to us) and dislike similar things (e.g. being criticised unfairly and failing at those same important tasks). In other areas of life, however, we differ markedly in what we want to happen and want not to happen. Thus, I may want Albion Rovers to be promoted next season from the Scottish Second Division, while you may be completely indifferent about this. You, on the other hand, may want to see a performance of Wagner's Ring Cycle which I might pay not to see! When we get our desires met, we will have positive feelings, at least initially, and when our desires are not met, we will generally experience negative feelings. This book is based on the idea, which I will develop later, that psychological health occurs in response to our unmet preferences when we experience negative feelings that are healthy, while psychological disturbance occurs in response to this same situation when we experience negative feelings that are unhealthy.

In this concise guide, I refer to situations where a client's preferences are not met as 'adversities' (Dryden, 2016). People can experience a variety of adversities in life and, in part, the type of adversity we face determines what feelings we experience. Please note the phrase 'in part' as it is critical, as I will make clear later.

Adversity

As I have just said, in this guide, I will call a situation where a client's preference has not, is not, may not or will not be met an *adversity*. This includes both situations where a client does not get what they want and situations where they get what they don't want. While anything can be an adversity for a client, the emotions that they experience point to the existence of a particular type of adversity. This is not to say that an adversity causes an emotion – far from it as you will soon see – but there is an association between different emotions and different adversities. So, if you are unsure about what kind of adversity a client is facing or thinks they are facing, one way to find out is to determine what emotion the client is experiencing. Table 1.1 lists a number of troublesome emotions and some of the adversities with which they are associated. I refer to such troublesome emotions as 'unhealthy negative emotions' (UNEs) in this guide (Dryden, 2012).[1]

What is important to bear in mind is that an adversity can represent what actually happened to a client or what they think has happened to them. The latter is known as an inference, and it is important to recognise that while the inferences that clients make may be accurate or inaccurate, they have an impact on them when they think they have experienced them. Table 1.1 outlines the UNEs that a client experiences when that impact is unconstructive and Table 1.2 outlines the healthy negative emotions (HNEs) that they experience when that impact is constructive (Dryden, 2012).

Rational Emotive Behaviour Therapy and Cognitive Behaviour Therapy

This guide is based on the therapy approach called 'Rational Emotive Behaviour Therapy' (REBT) which is a specific approach within the psychotherapy tradition known as 'Cognitive Behaviour Therapy' (CBT). There is a phrase attributable to Epictetus, the Greek Sage and Stoic philosopher which nicely encapsulates one of CBT's basic premises. It is: "People are disturbed not by things, but by their views of things". Thus, it is not the fact of the client's preferences not being met that disturbs them, but the view that they take of this situation. Now, when the

Table 1.1 Eight unhealthy negative emotions and some of their associated adversities

Unhealthy negative emotion	**Adversity**
Anxiety	• You are facing a threat to which you hold dear.
Depression	• You have experienced a significant loss. • You have significantly failed at something. • You and/or others have experienced an unfair plight.
Guilt	• You have broken one of your moral codes. • You have failed to live up to one of your moral codes. • You have hurt or harmed someone.
Shame	• You have fallen very short of your ideal. • Others have shown that they devalue you. • You have let down a social group with whom you closely identify. • A member of the social group with whom you closely identify has let down that group.
Hurt	• Others have neglected or betrayed you and you think you don't deserve this. • You are more invested in a relationship with someone than that person is with you.
Unhealthy anger	• Someone frustrates you, threatens you or disrespects you. • You have encountered an obstacle to an immediate goal or longer term objective. • Someone breaks one of your rules. • You break one of your own rules.
Jealousy	• Someone is threatening the relationship you have with a significant other. • You face uncertainty with respect to the above threat.
Unhealthy envy	• Someone has what you desire but do not have.

Table 1.2 Eight healthy negative emotions and some of their associated adversities

Healthy negative emotion	Adversity
Non-anxious concern	• You are facing a threat to what you hold dear.
Non-depressed sadness	• You have experienced a significant loss. • You have significantly failed at something. • You and/or others have experienced an unfair plight.
Guilt-free remorse	• You have broken one of your moral codes. • You have failed to live up to one of your moral codes. • You have hurt or harmed someone.
Shame-free disappointment	• You have fallen very short of your ideal. • Others have shown that they devalue you. • You have let down a social group with whom you closely identify. • A member of the social group with whom you closely identify has let down that group.
Hurt-free sorrow	• Others have neglected or betrayed you and you think you don't deserve this. • You are more invested in a relationship with someone than that person is with you.
Healthy anger	• Someone frustrates you, threatens you or disrespects you. • You have encountered an obstacle to an immediate goal or longer term objective. • Someone breaks one of your rules. • You break one of your own rules.
Non-jealous concern for your relationship	• Someone is threatening the relationship you have with a significant other. • You face uncertainty with respect to the above threat.
Healthy envy	• Someone has what you desire but do not have.

term 'view' is considered, it can be seen that it is quite a general term. This is fine if you want to get a general sense of what CBT is about as summed up by these formulae:

Things ≠ Disturbance
Things + Views = Disturbance

The role of attitudes

However, if you want to understand more precisely what REBT has to say about this topic, then I will need to use the term 'attitude', which is a little more precise. When I use the term 'attitude' here, I mean the evaluative stance that a client takes towards something, such as an adversity (remember that in this concise guide, an adversity occurs when a client does not get their preferences met). The position that I take in this book, then, is that it is the client's attitude that largely determines how they feel and respond to life's adversities. If you refer back to Table 1.1 and Table 1.2, you may have wondered what determines the client's differential response to the same adversities. This is a core point which I will develop later in this guide. For now, let me say that REBT's position is that when a client experiences an unhealthy negative emotion in the face of an adversity, they do so because they hold a set of *rigid and extreme* attitudes towards that adversity. And when they experience healthy negative emotions in the face of the same adversity, they do so because they hold a set of *flexible and non-extreme* attitudes towards the adversity. I will expand on this position below (Dryden, 2016).

As the above shows, a client has a choice of attitude towards experiencing life's adversities. While it is theoretically possible for the client to have a positive attitude or a neutral attitude towards an adversity, this is unrealistic. As such, I am not going to consider these two positions.[2] The two remaining options concerning the attitude that a client can choose to adopt towards facing an adversity can both be said to be negative in that they both indicate that an adversity is negative. The client is neither pleased that it happened nor are they indifferent. They care in the sense that they wish that it did not happen. Let's assume that the preference component of the client's attitude is this: "I wish that I had gotten the job that I applied for".

Rigid versus flexible attitudes

The two negative attitudes that remain for the client to choose from both contain this component. This makes clear what the client's preference is (in this case, to get the job that they applied for) and that, obviously, they prefer having their desire met. The two attitudes differ in that one is flexible, while the other is rigid. Let me first consider rigid attitudes.

Rigid attitudes

Rigid attitudes have two components. In the first component, the client makes clear what their preference is. I call this the 'preference' component. In the second component, the client asserts the idea that they must have their desire met. For this reason, I call this the 'demand' component. Thus:

> **Rigid attitude = 'Preference' component + 'Demand' component**
> *Example of rigid attitude = "I would have preferred to have got the job I applied for ('preference' component), and therefore I absolutely should have gotten it ('demand' component)".*

Flexible attitudes

Flexible attitudes also have two components. In the first component, as already noted, the client asserts or makes clear what their preference is. They want to have their desire met (in this case, again, to get the job that they applied for). This is again the client's 'preference' component. In the second component, however, the client makes clear that they recognise that they don't have to have their desire met. For this reason, I call this the 'anti-demand' component. Thus:

> **Flexible attitude = 'Preference' component + 'Anti-demand' component**
> *Example of flexible attitude = "I would have preferred to have got the job I applied for ('preference' component), but unfortunately, that does not mean that I absolutely should have gotten it ('anti-demand' component)".*

A brief overview of the consequences of rigid and flexible attitudes

When a client holds a rigid attitude towards an adversity (by asserting both their preference for having their desire met and their demand to have this desire met), then their responses to this adversity tend to be unconstructive and get them into deep psychological trouble. Not only are they facing an adversity, but they are also disturbing themself about this adversity. However, when the client holds a flexible attitude towards the same adversity (by asserting their preference for having their desire met, but without demanding that it has to be that way), they tend to deal constructively with the adversity. I will amplify on these two points presently. However, the vital issue to bear in mind is this. The client's preference is not what determines whether their attitude is healthy or not. What is crucial here is whether they keep their preference flexible (which is the defining feature of a healthy attitude) or whether they make it rigid (which is the defining feature of an unhealthy attitude).

The case of Frank

Let me demonstrate what I mean by taking the example of a client whom I will call 'Frank'. Frank likes his job and wants to get promoted in the new financial year. He can provide plenty of evidence why he wants this promotion. It will give him more money, he will have more exciting work to do, and he thinks that he may even impress his friends if he gets promoted. It transpired, however, that Frank did not get his preference met. He did not get promoted.

The importance of inferences

Now the fact of the matter is that Frank did not get his desired promotion, but as we shall see, it is possible for Frank to disturb himself about different aspects of this situation which are not factual features of the situation. Rather, they involve the person, in this case, Frank, making inferences, which are hunches that may be correct or incorrect, but which go beyond the data at hand. Here, I will discuss four such inferences that Frank could have made in this situation. In reality, while a person may make more than one inference in a situation like not getting a desired promotion, they will mainly disturb themself about one.

In this guide, I will assume that Frank makes the following inferences about him not getting his desired promotion:

- Not getting the desired promotion is **unfair**.
- Not getting the desired promotion represents **failure**.
- Not getting the desired promotion leads me to focus on the other person who got promotion and, in particular, on **me not having what the other person got**.
- Not getting the desired promotion leads me to focus on **others finding out about me not getting promoted and looking down on me**.

Frank holds a rigid attitude

If Frank made his basic attitude towards his unmet preference rigid, i.e., "I would have preferred to have been promoted, and therefore it absolutely should have happened", he would have felt bad about not being promoted and unhealthily so. Let's now see what would have happened if Frank held a rigid attitude towards different specific adversities within this general situation. I have put these specific adversities in bold.

- If Frank focused on the **perceived unfairness** of not being promoted and held a rigid attitude towards this (e.g. "I would have preferred to have been treated fairly, and therefore this absolutely should have happened"), he would have felt unhealthily angry rather than healthily angry about this. Consequently, if he communicated his unhealthy angry feelings to the appropriate person, he would have been aggressive and his attempts to correct the injustice would consequently have demonstrated lack of respect for the person. Thus, he would not have listened to that person's point of view and would have failed to understand what this viewpoint was. He would be likely not to give his best to his employer in his continuing role and may have gotten into trouble because of this. Finally, he may well have held a grudge if he continued to think he was unfairly treated.
- If Frank focused on his **failure** and held a rigid attitude towards this (e.g. "I would have preferred not to have failed, and therefore it absolutely should not have happened"), he would have felt depressed rather than sad about his failure. This would have prevented him from stepping back and considering reasons why he may have failed and thus he would have kept repeating any mistakes that may have led to this failure. He would have tried to banish thoughts of this failure from his mind without really managing to do so or would have dwelt on his previous failures and would have regarded *himself* as a failure. He would also have not applied for better jobs in other companies even if it meant furthering his career.
- If Frank focused on **not having what the other person got** (i.e. job promotion) and held a rigid attitude towards this (e.g. "I would have preferred to have what the other person got, and therefore I absolutely should have it"), he would have felt unhealthily envious rather than healthily envious when he focused on this imbalance. This would have led him to ruminate on this imbalance. He would have disparaged the other person and/or the promoted job to anyone who would listen to him and eventually these others would shun him rather than listen to

his endless negativity about the other person and/or the job that he failed to get.

- If Frank focused on the possibility of **others finding out about his failure to be promoted and looking down on him** and held a rigid attitude towards this (e.g. "I would prefer people not to look down on me for failing to be promoted, and therefore they must not do so"), he would have felt ashamed rather than disappointed about this should it occur. This would have led him to assume that it would happen and thus, he would take special care to hide his failure from others. This would then lead to him feeling increasingly tense with other people should they find out or should he let something slip. He would also tend to avoid these others if he could.

Frank holds a flexible attitude

If Frank kept his basic attitude towards his unmet preference flexible, i.e., "I would have preferred to have been promoted, but sadly and regretfully, that does not mean that it absolutely should have happened" he would have felt bad about not being promoted, but this time healthily so. Let's now see what would have happened if Frank held a flexible attitude towards the same specific adversities within this general situation as above. In what follows, Frank's specific adversity is again in bold.

- If Frank focused on the **perceived unfairness** of not being promoted and held a flexible attitude towards this (e.g. "I would have preferred to have been treated fairly, but sadly and regretfully, there is no reason why this absolutely should have happened"), the anger that he felt would have been healthy rather than unhealthy. Consequently, he would have communicated his feelings to the appropriate person and would have attempted to correct the injustice. These attempts would have been assertive and showed respect for the other person. Thus, Frank would also have listened to the other person's point of view, and if he understood this, he would have agreed to differ and continued to give his best to his employer in his continuing role. He would not have held a grudge even if he continued to think he was unfairly treated.
- If Frank focused on his **failure** and held a flexible attitude towards this (e.g. "I would have preferred not to have failed, but unfortunately it does not follow that this absolutely should not have happened"), he would have felt sad about his failure, but not depressed. This would have enabled him to step back and consider reasons why he may have failed and to resolve to implement what he learned from this reflective

exercise. He would have stayed focused on this failure and would not have dwelt on his previous failures and would certainly not have regarded himself as a failure which he may well have done if he had felt depressed because he held a rigid attitude about failing to get promoted. Also, if his attitude was flexible, he might have seriously considered applying for better jobs at other companies to further his career if opportunities for doing so at his present company were limited.

- If Frank focused on **not having what the other person got** (i.e. job promotion) and held a flexible attitude towards this (e.g. "I would have preferred to have what the other person got, but there is no reason why I absolutely should have it"), he would have felt healthily envious rather than unhealthily envious when he focused on this imbalance. This would have helped him to think creatively about what he could do to get what he wanted. He would have expressed his disappointment about not having what the other person got, but without disparaging the other person or the promoted job which he may well have done if he had felt unhealthily envious because he held a rigid attitude about what the other had that he desired, but lacked.
- If Frank focused on the possibility of **others finding out about his failure to be promoted and looking down on him** and held a flexible attitude towards this (e.g. "I would prefer people not to look down on me for failing to be promoted, but this does not mean that they must not do so"), he would have felt disappointed rather than ashamed about this should it occur. This would have led him to test out his inference that they would look down on him and to change this inference if he found no evidence to support it. He would also tend to mix with these people rather than avoid them.

The consequences of rigid and flexible attitudes

I made the point earlier that, in general, rigid attitudes held about adversity tend to yield consequences that are largely unconstructive, while flexible attitudes held about the same adversity tend to yield consequences that are largely constructive. These positions can be summed up as follows:

Adversity + Rigid attitude = Unhealthy consequences Adversity + Flexible attitude = Healthy consequences

There are four major types of consequences that stem from holding a rigid or flexible attitude. These consequences tend to be unhealthy when the client holds a rigid attitude and healthy when they hold a flexible attitude. These four types of consequences are:

- Secondary attitude consequences.
- Emotional consequences.
- Behavioural consequences.
- Other thinking consequences.

The consequences of rigid attitudes

When a client holds a rigid attitude towards an adversity, they experience a number of consequences which tend to be unhealthy. I will discuss the four major types of consequences here.

Secondary attitude consequences of rigid attitudes

Many of the ideas that appear in this book have been inspired by one of the grandfathers of CBT, Albert Ellis (1913–2007). Ellis (1994) argued, in particular, that when a client holds a rigid attitude, they are also likely to hold one or more extreme attitudes. These attitudes are called secondary attitudes in that they are deemed to stem from the client's rigid attitude. Ellis put forward three such secondary extreme attitudes. I will describe these one at a time and illustrate each with the case of Frank.

Awfulising attitude

Once a client holds a primary attitude towards an adversity, they also hold a secondary attitude that points to their evaluation of the adversity and its effect on their life. When the client's primary attitude is rigid, then their secondary attitude in this respect is likely to be extreme and indicate that they hold that the adversity and its impact on their life cannot be any worse. For this reason, this secondary extreme attitude is known as an 'awfulising'. Although this attitude is based on a reasonable evaluation of badness, when the client holds it they make this extreme and it is this extreme evaluation that colours their view of everything in their life and their future. They can't see any good in the bad, and they can't imagine transcending the adversity. It is as if their extreme evaluation of the adversity is going to define their whole life going forward. Phrases such as "It's awful" and "It's the end of the world" exemplify this extreme attitude.

BACK TO FRANK

If Frank held this extreme attitude towards the adversities associated with him not getting get promoted, it would be as follows:[3]

Adversity	**Rigid attitude**	**Secondary extreme attitude 1: Awfulising attitude**
Perceived unfairness	"I would have preferred to have been treated fairly, and therefore this absolutely should have happened."	"It is bad and therefore terrible to be treated unfairly."
Failure	"I would have preferred not to have failed to get promoted, and therefore it absolutely should not have happened."	"It is very regrettable and therefore awful that I failed to get promoted."
Not having what the other person got	"I would have preferred to have what the other person got, and therefore I absolutely should have it."	"It is very disadvantageous that the other person has what I want and therefore it is the end of the world."
Others finding out about my failure to be promoted and looking down on me	"I would prefer people not to look down on me for failing to be promoted, and therefore they must not do so."	"People looking down on me for failing to get promoted is bad, and nothing could be worse."

Discomfort intolerance attitude

Once a client holds a primary attitude towards an adversity, they also may hold a secondary attitude that points to their perceived ability to tolerate the adversity. When their primary attitude is rigid, then their secondary attitude in this respect is likely to be extreme and indicate that they hold that while it is a struggle, they cannot tolerate the adversity in question. For this reason, this secondary extreme attitude can be referred to as discomfort intolerance. When the client holds this attitude they tend to believe that they will disintegrate if they don't get away from the adversity or change it very quickly and that if they cannot get away from it or change it then they have no prospect of any happiness in any area of their life as long as the adversity continues to exist. In addition to the phrase "I can't tolerate it", the client may say, "I can't bear it", "It's intolerable", "It's unbearable", or "I can't endure it".

BACK TO FRANK

If Frank held this extreme attitude towards the adversities associated with him not getting promoted, it would be as follows:[4]

Adversity	**Rigid attitude**	**Secondary extreme attitude 2: Discomfort intolerance attitude**
Perceived unfairness	"I would have preferred to have been treated fairly, and therefore this absolutely should have happened."	"It's hard to bear being treated unfairly, and therefore I can't bear it."
Failure	"I would have preferred not to have failed to get promoted, and therefore it absolutely should not have happened."	"Failing to get promoted is not only difficult to bear, it is intolerable."
Not having what the other person got	"I would have preferred to have what the other person got, and therefore I absolutely should have it."	"It's a struggle, and therefore I can't stand it that the other person has what I want."
Others finding out about my failure to be promoted and looking down on me	"I would prefer people not to look down on me for failing to be promoted, and therefore they must not do so."	"It's difficult, and therefore I could not endure it if people looked down on me for failing to get promoted."

"Devaluation of self / others / life"

Once a client holds a primary attitude towards adversity, they also hold a secondary attitude about who or what is responsible for the adversity. When their primary attitude is rigid, then their secondary attitude in this respect is likely to be extreme and indicate a global negative evaluation of who or what they deem to be responsible. For this reason, this secondary extreme attitude involves devaluation of self, others or life. The client's secondary attitude begins with a negative evaluation of the relevant aspect, but then they overgeneralise and judge the whole by the part. For this reason, a devaluation attitude displays what philosophers refer to as the part-whole error.

BACK TO FRANK

If Frank held this extreme attitude about the adversities associated with him failing to get promoted, they would be as follows:[5]

Adversity	**Rigid attitude**	**Secondary extreme attitude 3: Devaluation attitude towards self/others/life**
Perceived unfairness	"I would have preferred to have been treated fairly, and therefore this absolutely should have happened."	*Others deemed to be responsible for the adversity* "The unfair decision my company made by not promoting me is bad and therefore my company is all bad for treating me unfairly."
Failure	"I would have preferred not to have failed to get promoted, and therefore it absolutely should not have happened."	*Self deemed to be responsible for the adversity* "Not getting promoted is bad in that it is a failure and proves, therefore, that I am a failure."
Not having what the other person got	"I would have preferred to have what the other person got, and therefore I absolutely should have it."	*Life deemed responsible for the adversity* "It is bad that the other person has what I want, and therefore life is bad for permitting this to happen."
Others finding out about my failure to be promoted and looking down on me	"I would prefer people not to look down on me for failing to be promoted, and therefore they must not do so."	*Self deemed to be responsible for the adversity* "People looking down on me for failing to get promoted is very unfortunate and proves that I am defective."

Emotional consequences of rigid attitudes

When the client holds a rigid attitude towards an adversity, then the emotions they experience tend to be negative and unhealthy.[6]

BACK TO FRANK

We can see what Frank felt when he held a rigid attitude towards each of the four specific adversities discussed:

Adversity	**Rigid attitude**	**Emotion**
Perceived unfairness	"I would have preferred to have been treated fairly, and therefore this absolutely should have happened."	Unhealthy anger
Failure	"I would have preferred not to have failed to get promoted, and therefore it absolutely should not have happened."	Depression
Not having what the other person got	"I would have preferred to have what the other person got, and therefore I absolutely should have it."	Unhealthy envy
Others finding out about my failure to be promoted and looking down on me	"I would prefer people not to look down on me for failing to be promoted, and therefore they must not do so."	Shame

Behavioural consequences of rigid attitudes

When a client holds a rigid attitude towards an adversity then what you do or feel like doing (known as action tendencies[7]) tends to be unconstructive.

BACK TO FRANK

We can see what Frank did when he held a rigid attitude about each of the four specific adversities discussed:

Adversity	Rigid attitude	Behaviour
Perceived unfairness	"I would have preferred to have been treated fairly, and therefore this absolutely should have happened."	• Aggressive, non-respectful communication and attempts to correct injustice. • Failure to listen to and understand the other's viewpoint. • Not giving best to the employer and getting into trouble because of this.
Failure	"I would have preferred not to have failed to get promoted, and therefore it absolutely should not have happened."	• Repeating mistakes that led to a failure to be promoted. • Not applying for better jobs at other companies.
Not having what the other person got	"I would have preferred to have what the other person got, and therefore I absolutely should have it."	• Disparaging the other person and/or the promoted job to others who will avoid him if this disparagement continues.
Others finding out about my failure to be promoted and looking down on me	"I would prefer people not to look down on me for failing to be promoted, and therefore they must not do so."	• Taking steps to hide his failure from others. • Avoiding others.

Other thinking consequences of rigid attitudes

When a client holds a rigid attitude towards an adversity, then the thinking they subsequently engage in – that stems from this attitude – tends to be highly distorted and skewed to the negative.[8] I will discuss how to help the client deal with such thinking as one component of a comprehensive approach to attitude change in Part 2 of this book.

BACK TO FRANK

We can see what subsequent thinking Frank engaged in when he held a rigid attitude about each of the four specific adversities discussed:

Adversity	**Rigid attitude**	**Subsequent thinking**
Perceived unfairness	"I would have preferred to have been treated fairly, and therefore this absolutely should have happened."	"Life is unfair."
Failure	"I would have preferred not to have failed to get promoted, and therefore it absolutely should not have happened."	"I'll never get promoted."
Not having what the other person got	"I would have preferred to have what the other person got, and therefore I absolutely should have it."	"I never wanted promotion anyway."
Others finding out about my failure to be promoted and looking down on me	"I would prefer people not to look down on me for failing to be promoted, and therefore they must not do so."	"People will always look down on me."

The consequences of flexible attitudes

When a client holds flexible attitudes towards adversities, they experience a number of consequences which tend to be healthy. I will discuss the four major types of consequences here.

Secondary attitude consequences of flexible attitudes

Albert Ellis (1994) argued that when a client holds a flexible attitude, they are also likely to hold one or more non-extreme attitudes. As with secondary extreme attitudes (discussed above), these non-extreme attitudes are called secondary attitudes in that are deemed to stem from the client's flexible attitude. Ellis put forward three secondary non-extreme attitudes. I will describe these one at a time and illustrate each with the case of Frank.

Non-awfulising attitude

There is an old American proverb that reflects the non-extreme attitude that things can almost always[9] be worse. It is this: "From the day you are born, till you ride in the hearse there is nothing so bad that it couldn't be worse". This non-extreme evaluation of an adversity, which is based on an evaluation of badness, is known as a non-awfulising attitude, allows the client to see good in the bad and enables them to see also that they can transcend the adversity however difficult this experience may seem. This non-extreme evaluation of the adversity prevents the client from defining their whole life going forward by the adversity's existence. Phrases such as "It's bad, but not awful" and "However bad it is, it's not the end of the world" exemplify this non-extreme attitude.

BACK TO FRANK

If Frank held this non-awfulising attitude towards the adversities associated with him failing to get promoted, they would be as follows:[10]

Adversity	**Flexible attitude**	**Secondary non-extreme attitude 1: Non-awfulising attitude**
Perceived unfairness	"I would have preferred to have been treated fairly, but sadly and regretfully, there is no reason why this absolutely should have happened."	"It is bad to be treated unfairly, but not terrible."
Failure	"I would have preferred not to have failed to get promoted, but unfortunately it does not follow that this absolutely should not have happened."	"It is unfortunate that I failed to get promoted, but it is not awful."
Not having what the other person got	"I would have preferred to have what the other person got, but there is no reason why I absolutely should have it."	"It is very disadvantageous, but not the end of the world that the other person has what I want."
Others finding out about my failure to be promoted and looking down on me	"I would prefer people not to look down on me for failing to be promoted, but this does not mean that they must not do so."	"People looking down on me for failing to get promoted would be very bad, but it could be worse."

Discomfort tolerance attitude

As I mentioned earlier, once a client holds a primary attitude about an adversity, they also hold a secondary attitude that points to their perceived ability to tolerate the adversity. When the client's primary attitude is flexible, then their secondary attitude in this respect is likely to be non-extreme and indicate that they believe that while it may be a struggle, they can tolerate the adversity in question, that it is worth it to them to do so and that they are going to do so. When the client holds this non-extreme attitude, they tend to believe that, although difficult, they can face the adversity and that if the adversity can be changed, they can strive to change it having given themself time to think about it and to select the best change strategy. If they cannot get away from the adversity or change it, then this discomfort tolerance attitude will help them to see that they can still experience happiness in their life. In addition to the phrase "It's a struggle but I can tolerate it", the client may say, "I can bear it", "It's tolerable", "It's bearable", or "I can endure it".

BACK TO FRANK

If Frank held this non-extreme attitude about the adversities associated with him failing to get promoted, they would be as follows:[11]

Adversity	**Flexible attitude**	**Secondary non-extreme attitude 2: Discomfort tolerance attitude**
Perceived unfairness	"I would have preferred to have been treated fairly, but sadly and regretfully, there is no reason why this absolutely should have happened."	"It's hard to bear being treated unfairly, but I can do so. It's worth it to me to do so, and I'm going to do so."
Failure	"I would have preferred not to have failed to get promoted, but unfortunately it does not follow that this absolutely should not have happened."	"It's in my interests to tolerate failing to get promoted. I can do so even though it's difficult and I'm going to do so."
Not having what the other person got	"I would have preferred to have what the other person got, but there is no reason why I absolutely should have it."	"I can stand it that the other person has what I want. It's a struggle to do so but worth it and I commit myself to standing it."

Adversity	**Flexible attitude**	**Secondary non-extreme attitude 2: Discomfort tolerance attitude**
Others finding out about my failure to be promoted and looking down on me	"I would prefer people not to look down on me for failing to be promoted, but this does not mean that they must not do so."	"It would be difficult, but if people looked down on me for failing to get promoted, I could endure it, and it would be in my interests to do so. Thus, I am going to do so."

Unconditional acceptance attitude towards self / others / life

Once a client holds a primary attitude towards an adversity, they also hold a secondary attitude towards who or what they deem to be responsible for the adversity. When the client's primary attitude is flexible then their secondary attitude, in this respect, is likely to be non-extreme. This involves a negative evaluation of behaviour or factors responsible for the adversity, but an unconditional acceptance of the person involved and/or of life, in general. For this reason, this secondary non-extreme attitude is known as 'unconditional acceptance of self/others/life'.

BACK TO FRANK

If Frank held an acceptance attitude towards the adversities associated with him failing to get promoted, they would be as follows:[12]

Adversity	**Flexible attitude**	**Secondary non-extreme attitude 3: "Unconditional acceptance of self/others/life."**
Perceived unfairness	"I would have preferred to have been treated fairly, but sadly and regretfully, there is no reason why this absolutely should have happened."	*Others deemed to be responsible for the adversity* "The unfair decision my company made by not promoting me is bad, but the whole of the company is not all bad. It is a complex mixture of good, bad and neutral aspects."

Adversity	**Flexible attitude**	**Secondary non-extreme attitude 3: "Unconditional acceptance of self/others/life."**
Failure	"I would have preferred not to have failed to get promoted, but unfortunately it does not follow that this absolutely should not have happened."	*Self deemed to be responsible for the adversity* "It's bad that I failed to get promoted, but I am not a failure for failing to get promoted. I'm a fallible human being capable of success and failure."
Not having what the other person got	"I would have preferred to have what the other person got, but there is no reason why I absolutely should have it."	*Life deemed responsible for the adversity* "Life is bad in this respect for allowing the other person to have what I want, but it is not bad in entirety. It's a complex mix of good, bad and neutral aspects."
Others finding out about my failure to be promoted and looking down on me	"I would prefer people not to look down on me for failing to be promoted, but this does not mean that they must not do so."	*Self deemed to be responsible for the adversity* "People looking down on me for failing to get promoted is very unfortunate but does not prove that I am defective. I am human, not defective."

Emotional consequences of flexible attitudes

When a client holds a flexible attitude about an adversity, then the emotions they experience tend to be negative and healthy.[13]

BACK TO FRANK

We can see what Frank felt when he held a flexible attitude about each of the four specific adversities discussed:

Adversity	Flexible attitude	Emotion
Perceived unfairness	"I would have preferred to have been treated fairly, but sadly and regretfully, there is no reason why this absolutely should have happened."	Healthy anger
Failure	"I would have preferred not to have failed to get promoted, but unfortunately it does not follow that this absolutely should not have happened."	Sadness
Not having what the other person got	"I would have preferred to have what the other person got, but there is no reason why I absolutely should have it."	Healthy envy
Others finding out about my failure to be promoted and looking down on me	"I would prefer people not to look down on me for failing to be promoted, but this does not mean that they must not do so."	Disappointment

Behavioural consequences of flexible attitudes

When a client holds a flexible attitude about an adversity then what they do or feel like doing (known as action tendencies[14]) tends to be constructive.

BACK TO FRANK

Referring back to the case Frank we can see what Frank did when he held a flexible attitude about each of the four specific adversities discussed:

Adversity	Flexible attitude	Behaviour
Perceived unfairness	"I would have preferred to have been treated fairly, but sadly and regretfully, there is no reason why this absolutely should have happened."	• Assertive, respectful communication and attempts to correct injustice. • Listening to and understanding the other's viewpoint. • Giving my best to my employer.

Adversity	Flexible attitude	Behaviour
Failure	"I would have preferred not to have failed to get promoted, but unfortunately it does not follow that this absolutely should not have happened."	• Learning from mistakes that led to failure to be promoted. • Applying for better jobs at other companies, if appropriate.
Not having what the other person got	"I would have preferred to have what the other person got, but there is no reason why I absolutely should have it."	• Taking steps to get what the other has if this is truly what one wants. • Expressing disappointment to others without disparaging the other person and/or the promoted job to these others.
Others finding out about my failure to be promoted and looking down on me	"I would prefer people not to look down on me for failing to be promoted, but this does not mean that they must not do so."	• Facing and mixing with others. • Being open about his failure to others.

Other thinking consequences of flexible attitudes

When a client holds a flexible attitude about an adversity, then the thinking they subsequently engage in that stems from this attitude tends to be realistic and balanced.[15]

BACK TO FRANK

We can see what subsequent thinking Frank engaged in when he held a rigid attitude about each of the four specific adversities discussed:

Adversity	Flexible attitude	Subsequent thinking
Perceived unfairness	"I would have preferred to have been treated fairly, but sadly and regretfully, there is no reason why this absolutely should have happened."	"This aspect of life may be unfair, but life as a whole can be fair and unfair."

Adversity	Flexible attitude	Subsequent thinking
Failure	"I would have preferred not to have failed to get promoted, but unfortunately it does not follow that this absolutely should not have happened."	"It may be harder than I thought it would be to get promoted, but that does not mean that I will never get promoted."
Not having what the other person got	"I would have preferred to have what the other person got, but there is no reason why I absolutely should have it."	"I did want a promotion, and it's disappointing not to get it, but I can still enjoy other things that I have."
Others finding out about my failure to be promoted and looking down on me	"I would prefer people not to look down on me for failing to be promoted, but this does not mean that they must not do so."	"It's doubtful that people will always look down on me. One or two might, but most won't."

In this part of the guide, I have covered the basic REBT position concerning the attitudes clients hold towards life's adversities when they respond in a disturbed way to these adversities. I also discussed what alternative attitudes clients need to develop to respond healthily and realistically to the same adversities. In Part 2 of this concise guide, I will discuss how clients can be helped to change the unhealthy attitudes that underpin their disturbed reactions to the adversities that they face in life so that they can deal healthily with them.

Notes

1 The roots of this approach can be found in Beck (1976).
2 To hold a positive attitude towards an adversity, a client would be pleased that it happened and to hold a neutral attitude towards the adversity, they would genuinely not care whether it happened or not.
3 Please note that Frank's secondary extreme attitudes, known as awfulising attitudes are, in each case, derived from his rigid attitudes.
4 Please note that Frank's secondary extreme attitudes, known as discomfort intolerance attitudes are, in each case, derived from his rigid attitudes.
5 Please note that Frank's secondary extreme attitudes, known as devaluation attitudes towards self/others/life are, in each case, derived from his rigid attitudes.

6 See Appendix 1 for a full list of unhealthy negative emotions, what determines them and their behavioural and cognitive correlates.
7 An action tendency represents what we feel like doing or an urge to act in a given situation. It may or may not result in overt behaviour. See Appendix 1 for a list of the action tendencies and behaviours associated with each of the unhealthy negative emotions listed.
8 See Appendix 2 for a full list of these inferential distortions. Also see Appendix 1 for the types of inferential distortions that accompany unhealthy negative emotions.
9 Note the use of the phrase 'almost always' here. The word 'always' is extreme and would stem from a rigid attitude. 'Almost always' is realistic and stems from a flexible attitude. It allows for the possibility that the worst may happen and cannot be worse, however unlikely this is.
10 Please note that Frank's secondary non-extreme attitudes, known as non-awfulising attitudes are, in each case, derived from his flexible attitudes.
11 Please note that Frank's secondary non-extreme attitudes, known as discomfort tolerance attitudes are, in each case, derived from his flexible attitudes.
12 Please note that Frank's secondary non-extreme attitudes, known as unconditional acceptance attitudes towards self/others/life are, in each case, derived from his flexible attitude.
13 See Appendix 1 for a full list of healthy negative emotions, what determines them and their behavioural and cognitive correlates.
14 As mentioned earlier, an action tendency represents what we feel like doing or an urge to act in a given situation. It may or may not result in overt behaviour. See Appendix 1 for a list of the action tendencies and behaviours associated with each of the healthy negative emotions listed.
15 See Appendix 2 for a full list of these realistic and balanced inferences. Also see Appendix 1 for the types of such inferences that accompany healthy negative emotions.

Part 2

Helping clients change their attitudes towards adversity

> The greatest discovery of my generation is that human beings can alter lives by their attitudes.
>
> (William James)

In this part of the book, I discuss how therapists can help clients to stand back and examine their rigid/extreme attitudes in the face of adversity and the flexible/non-extreme alternatives to these attitudes.

In using these methods, clients will first understand that their rigid/extreme attitudes are unhelpful, inconsistent with reality and don't make logical sense, while their flexible/non-extreme alternative attitudes are helpful, consistent with reality and do make logical sense. However, in order for such understanding to make a real difference to clients' lives, they have to integrate them into their belief system through the regular application of a variety of cognitive-behavioural methods, many of which I describe and illustrate with reference to the case study.

Finally, I discuss how clients can respond constructively to a variety of obstacles to constructive attitude change.

Introduction

Once clients have been helped to understand the detrimental influence that holding rigid and extreme attitudes towards adversity have on their responses to such adversity and the beneficial influence that flexible and non-extreme attitudes could have on the way they respond, then the question is how can they be helped to change their rigid and extreme attitudes to their flexible and non-extreme alternatives? There are a number of ways of doing this, and I will now discuss them. Given that this is a concise guide, I will focus on some of the most common methods employed in REBT, but I want to stress that therapists should be encouraged to use their ingenuity and creativity in facilitating the attitude change process. Part 2 of this guide is divided into two. First, I will show how clients can be helped to gain what Albert Ellis (1963) called 'intellectual insight' into understanding why their rigid and extreme attitudes are problematic and why their flexible and non-extreme alternatives are non-problematic. While such insight is important, on its own it is insufficient to promote attitude change and ***does not*** impact constructively on their emotions behaviour and subsequent thinking. What is needed is for clients to gain what Ellis (1963) called 'emotional insight' which ***does*** impact constructively on their emotions, behaviour and subsequent thinking. This latter insight results from clients taking active and regular steps to deepen their conviction in their developing flexible and non-extreme attitudes towards adversity. Then, I discuss a variety of techniques that are designed to help clients gain such emotional insight.

Understanding-oriented techniques to promote intellectual insight

In this section, I will discuss a variety of cognitive or thinking techniques designed to help clients understand why their rigid and extreme attitudes towards adversity are problematic and conversely why their alternative flexible and non-extreme attitudes to the same adversity are beneficial. As I stressed above, intellectual insight is necessary, but not sufficient to promote constructive attitude change.

Have the client examine attitudes in pairs

This technique involves the client taking their attitudes in pairs and examining them from three different standpoints (DiGiuseppe, 1991): the true-false standpoint; the sense-nonsense standpoint; and the healthy-unhealthy standpoint.[1]

The true-false standpoint

When the client adopts this standpoint, they consider which of their attitudes is true and which is false.

The sense-nonsense standpoint

When the client adopts this standpoint, they consider which of their attitudes makes sense and is logical and which does not make sense and is illogical.

The healthy-unhealthy standpoint

When the client adopts this standpoint, they consider the consequences of holding the respective attitudes. This calls on the client to reflect on the question, which of their attitudes has healthy, helpful or constructive consequences and which has unhealthy, unhelpful or unconstructive consequences.

Once a client has made their choice then they are encouraged to reflect on and state their reasons. The therapist's major role in this process is to correct any misconceptions revealed and to suggest other reasons in favour of flexible/non-extreme attitudes and against rigid/extreme attitudes.

Encourage the client to make a commitment towards their flexible / non-extreme attitudes

After the client has engaged with the process of considering and reflecting on their rigid/extreme and flexible/non-extreme attitudes as above, they are in a position to make a commitment concerning which to strengthen and which to weaken and to be clear on the reasoning behind their choice. If all has gone to plan the client will make a commitment to strengthen the latter and weaken the former and be able to articulate clear reasons why.

BACK TO FRANK

Let me show you what I mean. Let me take one of Frank's rigid attitudes discussed in the first part of this short guide and its flexible alternative. For illustrative purposes, I have chosen Frank's rigid and flexible attitudes towards the unfairness that happened to him when he failed to get promoted. Table 2.1 outlines how Frank used the above three standpoints to examine his rigid and flexible attitudes towards unfairness. It also gives Frank an opportunity to say which attitude he would like to commit to strengthening and why.

Ask the client which attitude they would teach their children

A variant of the above foundational attitude change technique is for the client to take their attitude pair and imagine that they were going to teach a group of older children for whom they had responsibility why they should assume and develop the flexible/non-extreme attitude towards unfairness and not the rigid/extreme attitude. Which arguments

Table 2.1 How Frank examined his rigid and flexible attitudes towards unfairness

Rigid attitude about unfairness	**Flexible attitude about unfairness**
"I would have preferred to have been treated fairly and therefore this absolutely should have happened."	"I would have preferred to have been treated fairly, but sadly and regretfully, there is no reason why this absolutely should have happened."

Which attitude is true and which is false and why?

This attitude is false. While it is true that my preference is not to be treated unfairly, it is false to say that this absolutely should not have happened to me. The fact that it did happen to me proves that this rigid conclusion is false. It is false no matter how much I deserve to be treated fairly.	This attitude is true. First, it is true that my preference is not to be treated unfairly and second, it is also true that it does not mean that this absolutely should not have happened to me. The fact that it did happen to me can be incorporated into this attitude.

Which attitude makes sense and which does not make sense and why?

This attitude does not make sense as it is illogical to conclude that being treated unfairly must not happen to me just because I have a preference for it not to happen to me.	This attitude does make sense since both parts of it are not rigid and therefore the non-rigid conclusion follows logically from the non-rigid preference.

Which attitude is healthy for me and which is unhealthy and why?

This rigid attitude is unhealthy for me as it tends to lead to extreme attitudes, unhealthy negative emotions, unconstructive behaviour and highly distorted thinking.	This flexible attitude is healthy for me as it tends to lead to non-extreme attitudes, healthy negative emotions, constructive behaviour and balanced thinking.

Which attitude do I want to develop and which do I want to weaken and why?	
I want to develop my flexible attitude about fairness as it recognises the importance that I give to fairness, but does not make a dogma out of it. Being flexible will help me to ride the waves of adversity when I face unfair treatment and help me to address it without disturbing myself about it. Thus, it will help me think clearly about what I want to do to address the issue with my boss and also help me engage in a productive dialogue with them.	I want to weaken my rigid attitude because it does not just show how important fairness is to me, it shows that I am dogmatic about this good quality. When I am dogmatic about not being treated fairly, I am in a black and white, I am right, you are wrong state of mind, which leads to disturbed feelings and interferes with my ability to be objective about what to do about addressing the unfairness that I face. Such rigidity will also interfere with my ability to engage in a productive dialogue with my boss.

would they use and why? In Table 2.2, I outline what I would say on this matter to a group of older children for whom I had responsibility.

Techniques to promote emotional insight: Helping clients to develop conviction in their flexible and non-extreme attitudes

Once the client has committed themself to develop their flexible attitude,[2] they need to be helped to engage in a number of activities that will help them to strengthen their flexible attitude and weaken their rigid attitude.

Cognitive techniques

I will begin with a range of cognitive techniques designed to promote emotional insight which is, if you recall, insight which ***does*** impact constructively on the client's emotions, behaviour and subsequent thinking.

The rigid-flexible dialogue

One such activity involves the client giving expression to both the rigid and flexible attitudes about the adversity in question where they engage these different attitudes in a dialogue with one another. Given that the client has already committed themself to develop the flexible attitude,

Table 2.2 Helping children to choose between a rigid attitude and a flexible attitude about unfairness

Rigid attitude towards unfairness	**Flexible attitude towards unfairness**
"I would have preferred to have been treated fairly and therefore this absolutely should have happened."	"I would have preferred to have been treated fairly, but sadly and regretfully, there is no reason why this absolutely should have happened."

When something happens to you that you consider to be unfair, this is obviously a bad thing and, of course, you would much prefer to be treated fairly. No matter what anybody says to you, unfairness is bad and you are going to feel badly about it. It is neither healthy for you to have neutral feelings about the unfairness nor to feel good about it happening.

However, while you don't have a choice of feeling badly about the unfairness, there is one area where you do have a choice.

You can choose to feel badly about the unfairness but healthily so or to feel badly about it, but unhealthily so.

Remember you can't realistically choose to feel good about the unfairness because to do so you would have to believe: "I want to be treated unfairly and it is good that this has happened". This is nonsense. Also, you can't realistically choose to feel neutral about the unfairness because to do so you would have to believe: "It doesn't matter to me whether I am treated fairly or unfairly". Obviously it does matter to you and you prefer not to be treated unfairly.

So, first, let's see what is involved when you choose to feel badly about the unfairness that has happened to you, but healthily so.

1. You acknowledge that what you deem to be unfair has happened to you and you hold the following attitude towards it: "I would prefer it if the unfairness had not happened to me, but sadly I am not immune from it happening and also sadly there is no law of the universe decreeing that it absolutely should not have happened to me, no matter how much I deserve to be treated fairly rather than unfairly".
2. What you are doing here is acknowledging that just because you want the unfairness not to happen to you, it does not follow that it must not happen to you. This attitude is flexible because it incorporates your preference and also the idea that you don't have to have your preference met.
3. This flexible attitude will help you to face the unfairness and to deal with it while feeling badly, but healthily so.

4. This flexible attitude will also help you to put the unfairness into perspective and to realise that there may be some good to come out of the bad and that you can get on with your life even if you can't change things.
5. But most importantly, this flexible attitude will help you to think clearly about what to do about the unfairness and help you to execute your selected plan of action free from the presence of unhealthy negative emotions

Now let's see what is involved in choosing to feel badly about the unfairness that has happened to you, but, this time, unhealthily so.

1. You focus on what you deem to be the unfairness that has happened to you and you hold the following attitude towards it: "I would prefer it if the unfairness had not happened to me and therefore it absolutely should not have happened, particularly as I deserve to be treated fairly rather than unfairly".
2. What you are doing here is stating that because you want the unfairness not to happen to you, it follows that it must not happen to you. This attitude is rigid because you try, in your mind, to eliminate the possibility of being treated unfairly when the reality is that you have been treated unfairly. This rigid attitude, therefore, is against reality.
3. This rigid attitude will tend to interfere with you facing the unfairness and get in the way of you dealing with it in a constructive manner.
4. This rigid attitude will also prevent you from putting the unfairness into perspective and it will lead you to conclude, wrongly, that no good can possibly come out of the bad and that you can't get on with your life as long as the unfairness exists.
5. But most importantly this rigid attitude will affect markedly your ability to think clearly about what to do about the unfairness and lead you to take impulsive action in a bid to get rid of your unhealthy negative feelings.

Now you are in a position to choose: If you want to feel badly about unfairness, but healthily so, you can do so by taking your preference about not being treated unfairly and keeping it flexible. However, if you wish to feel badly about unfairness, but unhealthily so, you can do so by taking your preference about not being treated unfairly and making it rigid. The choice is yours.

the dialogue is purposive: the goal is, as noted above, to find arguments that will strengthen the client's conviction in their flexible attitude and to find compelling arguments in response to those used by their rigid 'voice' so that they can weaken their conviction in their rigid belief. As will be shown in Table 2.3, this technique involves the client going back and forth until they have silenced their rigid 'voice'. This can be done on paper (as in Table 2.3) or verbally, out loud. The latter approach has been called 'externalisation of voices' technique by David Burns (1980).

Table 2.3 Frank's use of the rigid-flexible dialogue technique

Flexible voice	Rigid voice
I would have preferred to have been treated fairly, but sadly and regretfully, there is no reason why this absolutely should have happened.	
	Yes, but I really did not deserve to be denied promotion, I really worked hard for it and therefore I absolutely should have gotten it.
There is no doubt that I worked really hard for the promotion and in an ideal world, I would have gotten it, but this is not an ideal world. Therefore, while ideally I should have gotten it, in reality there is no reason why I absolutely should have gotten it. This is consistent with reality as I did not get it.	
	I must have upset someone, otherwise I would have been promoted. It's just so unfair and it really shouldn't be that way.
Well, I may have upset someone, but also that is just what I would think if I am rigid about not being treated unfairly. I may not have upset anyone and those deciding who gets promotion and who doesn't may have seen things differently from me. But even if it is very unfair, I am not immune from unfairness and sadly nor do I have to be. If, objectively, I conclude that I have been discriminated against, I can make a formal complaint, but I will only do so when I am flexible in my attitude about what happened not when I am rigid about it.	

When the client uses the verbal dialogue version of the technique, they might find it useful to record the dialogue for later review. In employing this technique, it is important that the client responds effectively to all the arguments that they make when using their rigid 'voice'. Otherwise, they will retain those arguments which will limit the extent that they will develop their flexible attitude.

Another variant of this activity to deepen conviction in flexible/non-extreme attitudes and weaken conviction in rigid/extreme attitudes is through chairwork (see Kellogg, 2015 for a discussion of chairwork which is beyond the scope of this concise guide).

BACK TO FRANK

Table 2.3 shows how Frank used this technique as part of the process of strengthening his flexible attitude about being treated unfairly and weakening his rigid attitude about the same adversity.

Help the client identify and respond to doubts, reservations and objections

As the client strives to strengthen their conviction in their flexible attitude towards adversity and weaken their conviction in the corresponding rigid attitude, they may find themself resisting this process. This may well be due to the fact that they may have some doubts, reservations and objections (DROs) about operating according to the flexible version of their attitude as opposed to the rigid version. This also applies to the three non-extreme attitudes that are derived from the primary flexible attitude and the corresponding three extreme attitudes that are derived from the primary rigid attitude.

Table 2.4 lists the main DROs that clients have about surrendering their allegiance to their rigid and derived extreme attitudes and working towards developing their allegiance to their corresponding flexible and derived non-extreme beliefs. See Dryden (2001) for an extended discussion of this issue.

BACK TO FRANK

Table 2.5 shows how Frank responded to the DROs that he identified that he had about developing a set of flexible and non-extreme attitudes about being treated unfairly rather than operating on a corresponding set of rigid and extreme attitudes about the same adversity.

Table 2.4 Doubts, reservations and objections (DROs) to developing the flexible and derived non-extreme attitudes and relinquishing the rigid and derived extreme attitudes and suggestions on how to respond to them

Attitude pairing	**Doubt, reservation, objection (DRO) to developing the flexible and derived non-extreme attitudes and relinquishing the rigid and derived extreme attitudes**	**Response to the doubt, reservation and objection**
Rigid vs flexible attitude	• My rigid attitude motivates me to change the adversity more than my flexible attitude does.	• Both of these attitudes are based on the desire for the adversity not to exist. This desire creates motivation to change the adversity. When I make this desire rigid, I create emotional disturbance which interferes with this motivation which does not happen with my flexible attitude.
	• My rigid attitude shows that it is very important that I not experience the adversity, while my flexible attitude indicates a lower level of importance in this respect.	• It is the desire part of both attitudes that indicates the level of importance.
	• My rigid attitude indicates strength of feeling, while my flexible attitude is wishy-washy.	• Again, it's the desire part of both attitudes that indicates my strength of feeling, so my flexible attitude is not wishy-washy when compared to my rigid attitude.
	• If I refuse to permit the possibility of the adversity happening as in my rigid attitude than it is less likely to happen than if I allow for the possibility of it happening as in my flexible attitude.	• This is child-like magical thinking. It's like saying that if I close my eyes the world disappears. Whatever attitude I hold has no effect on whether or not the adversity happens.

Extreme vs non-extreme attitude #1 • **Awfulising attitude vs non-awfulising attitude**	• My extreme attitude here indicates the seriousness of the adversity while my non-extreme attitude makes light of it.	• Both of these attitudes are based on the same evaluation of badness and thus my non-extreme attitude does not make light of the adversity.
	• My extreme attitude here protects me from threat, while my non-extreme attitude needlessly exposes me to it.	• It is true that when I hold the extreme attitude it protects me from threat in the sense that I will avoid it. In doing so I am not dealing with it effectively which is actually what happens when I hold the non-extreme attitude.
Extreme vs non-extreme attitude #2 • **Discomfort intolerance attitude vs discomfort tolerance attitude**	• My extreme attitude will spare me from facing up to the adversity, while my non-extreme attitude leads me to put up with it.	• Again my extreme attitude leads to sparing me pain by avoidance. My non-extreme attitude will lead me to tolerate the presence of the adversity, but not in the passive way implied here. It will help me to change the adversity if it can be changed and to adjust constructively if it can't.
	• My extreme attitude helps me to avoid emotional pain. My non-extreme attitude will expose me to more emotional pain. Therefore, I am reluctant to give up my extreme attitude in favour of my non-extreme attitude.	• It is true that my extreme attitude will help me avoid emotional pain in the short-term by leading me to avoid the adversity, but it will not help me to deal with it effectively. When I hold my non-extreme attitude I will still feel badly, but my emotions will be healthy and help me to change the adversity if it can be changed and to adjust constructively if it can't be changed.

(*continued*)

Table 2.4 (Cont.)

Attitude pairing	Doubt, reservation, objection (DRO) to developing the flexible and derived non-extreme attitudes and relinquishing the rigid and derived extreme attitudes	Response to the doubt, reservation and objection
Extreme vs non-extreme attitude #3 • **Devaluation of self/others/life vs unconditional acceptance of self/others/life**	• Unconditionally accepting myself means that I don't need to change aspects of myself that I am not happy with or that I can't do so. Devaluing myself, on the other hand, motivates me to change. Therefore, adopting an unconditional self-acceptance attitude discourages personal change, while keeping my self-devaluation attitude encourages such change.	• Actually, the opposite is probably true. Unconditional self-acceptance means that I acknowledge that I am a complex, fallible human being with good, bad and neutral parts, so when I accept myself I am not complacent and can focus on parts of myself that I want to change and work to change them. When I devalue myself I am making a global negative rating of my 'self' which tends to discourage rather than encourage personal change.
	• Adopting an unconditional other-acceptance attitude means that I am condoning that person's bad behaviour. Devaluing that person shows that I am not condoning his (in this case) behaviour.	• The difference between these two attitudes is not in condoning vs non-condoning bad behaviour. Holding both leads to the person to not condone such behaviour. The difference lies in the attitude taken to the other: unconditional acceptance of the other versus condemnation of the other.

Table 2.5 Frank's doubts, reservations and objections (DROs) to developing flexible and derived non-extreme attitudes towards perceived unfairness and relinquishing the rigid and derived extreme attitudes about the same adversity and how he responded to them

Attitude pairing	**Frank's doubt, reservation, objection (DRO) to developing his flexible and derived non-extreme attitudes about being treated unfairly and relinquishing his rigid and derived extreme attitudes about the same adversity**	**Frank's response to the doubt, reservation and objection**
Rigid vs flexible attitude **"I would have preferred to have been treated fairly and therefore this absolutely should have happened"** **vs** **"I would have preferred to have been treated fairly, but sadly and regretfully, there is no reason why this absolutely should have happened"**	• My rigid attitude motivates me to take a stand against injustice while my flexible attitude leads me to tolerate it.	• Actually, both of these attitudes will lead me to take a stand against injustice. However, my flexible attitude encourages me to take such a stand free from the dysfunctional constraints of emotional disturbance which is a feature of my rigid attitude.
	• My rigid attitude indicates a strong moral position, while my flexible attitude seems more relaxed in its moral position. I want to maintain a strong moral perspective on this issue.	• The moral position is outlined in my desire standpoint which is common to both attitudes and thus equally strong in both. The difference is with respect to reality. If it was true that I absolutely should have been promoted, I would have been. My flexible attitude is strong in moral conviction and realistic in the sense that there is no law decreeing that I absolutely should have been promoted, no matter how just or fair this would have been.

(*continued*)

Table 2.5 (Cont.)

Attitude pairing	**Frank's doubt, reservation, objection (DRO) to developing his flexible and derived non-extreme attitudes about being treated unfairly and relinquishing his rigid and derived extreme attitudes about the same adversity**	**Frank's response to the doubt, reservation and objection**
Extreme vs non-extreme attitude #1 • **Awfulising attitude vs non-awfulising attitude** **"It is bad to be treated unfairly, and therefore it is terrible"** **vs** **"It is bad to be treated unfairly, but not terrible"**	• My extreme awfulising attitude here indicates the seriousness of the unfairness, while my non-extreme non-awfulising attitude makes light of it.	• Both of these attitudes are based on the same evaluation of badness and thus my non-extreme non-awfulising attitude does not make light of the unfairness. It just takes the 'horror' out of it.
Extreme vs non-extreme attitude #2 • **Discomfort intolerance attitude vs discomfort tolerance attitude**	• My extreme discomfort intolerance attitude will spare me from facing up to the adversity, while my non-extreme discomfort tolerance attitude leads me to put up with it.	• Again my extreme discomfort intolerance attitude leads to sparing me pain by avoidance. My non-extreme discomfort tolerance attitude will lead me to tolerate the presence of the adversity, but not in the passive way implied here. It will help me to change the adversity if it can be changed and to adjust constructively if it can't.

"It's hard to bear being treated unfairly and therefore I can't bear it" **vs** **"It's hard to bear being treated unfairly, but I can do so and it's worth it to me to do so"**	• My extreme discomfort intolerance attitude helps me to avoid emotional pain. My non-extreme discomfort tolerance attitude will expose me to more emotional pain. Therefore, I am reluctant to give up my extreme discomfort intolerance attitude in favour of my non-extreme discomfort tolerance attitude.	• It is true that my extreme discomfort intolerance attitude will help me avoid emotional pain in the short-term by leading me to avoid the adversity, but it will not help me to deal with it effectively. When I hold my non-extreme discomfort tolerance attitude I will still feel badly, but my emotions will be healthy and help me to change the adversity if it can be changed and to adjust constructively if it can't be changed.
Extreme vs non-extreme attitude #3 • **Devaluation of self/others/life vs Unconditional acceptance of self/others/life** **"The unfair decision my company made by not promoting me is bad and therefore my company is all bad for treating me unfairly"** **vs** **"The unfair decision my company made by not promoting me is bad, but the whole of the company is not all bad. It is a complex mixture of good, bad and neutral aspects"**	• If I think that my company is a complex mixture of good, bad and neutral aspects, then I won't be vigilant for future bad behaviour from them. But if I think that they are all bad, I will be vigilant and prevent bad things from happening to me.	• My extreme life-devaluating attitude won't just lead me to be vigilant for future bad behaviour from my company, it will lead me to be hypervigilant for such behaviour and edit out or rationalise away future good behaviour from my company. My unconditional life-acceptance attitude, on the other hand, will lead me to be vigilant, but not hypervigilant for future bad behaviour from my company, but will also lead me to acknowledge and give credit for their future good behaviour.

Behavioural techniques

In this section, I will discuss the role of behavioural techniques in attitude change.

Encourage the client to make a commitment to act

Up to now in this part, I have discussed what are basically thinking strategies to encourage the client to change their rigid and extreme attitudes about adversity to their flexible and non-extreme equivalents. I regard these thinking strategies as important, but usually insufficient to effect such change. They are like foundations without which any housing structure would be fragile, but on their own, they will not provide the client with a place to live. Once the client has laid the foundations for attitude change, it is important that they take action, and do so *with repetition* in order to enable such change to take root.

Agreeing to take action is quite easy, but actually taking action is a different matter. So, it may be helpful for the client to make a commitment to take action which is in the service of attitude change. Some clients, like Frank, prefer to make a private commitment to take action while others find making a public commitment useful. Encourage the client to think carefully about making such a commitment and if they think that it could be helpful to them, encourage them to do so and express it in a form that will be most useful to them in taking action.

Encourage the client to make their attitudes, behaviour, talk and associated thinking work in harmony

As noted by Mahatma Gandhi, "happiness is when what you think, what you say and what you do are in harmony". This is also true of psychological health. When a client takes action in the service of facilitating attitude change, it is important that they make their behaviour consistent with the flexible and/or non-extreme attitudes that they are in the process of developing and with the thinking that is associated with it. Then, when the client discusses related matters with people, it is useful for them to make what they say consistent with the attitudes that they are working to strengthen. In this way, all systems are firing in the same direction. When the client adds repetition into the mix then they will find that in facing their adversity, the more they act, think and talk in ways that are consistent with their developing flexible and/or non-extreme attitudes and in ways that are inconsistent with their rigid and extreme attitudes, the more they will deepen their conviction in their flexible and/or non-extreme attitudes. And the more this happens, the more their feelings will change from unhealthy negative emotions to healthy negative emotions.

BACK TO FRANK

Frank resolved to act, think and talk in ways that were consistent with his flexible and non-extreme attitudes about the unfairness of not getting promoted. He told his boss that while he thought it was unfair that he was passed over for promotion, he was sure that his company had reason to do so and he requested knowing what these reasons were. When telling his friends about not being promoted he agreed with them that it was unfair that he was not promoted and that this unfairness was bad, but much to their surprise, he corrected them when they told him that it was awful and that life was unfair for permitting this unfairness and explained why he disagreed with these notions.

Other methods and principles

In addition to cognitive and behavioural methods of attitude change, there are a variety of other relevant methods and principles that clients can use in the service of such change.

Use imagery rehearsal

As humans, clients have the capacity to imagine past events, current events and possible future events in their mind's eve. This can be for better or for worse. When it is for worse, the client focuses on an adversity and implicitly rehearses the rigid and/or extreme attitude that they hold about the adverse nature of that event and experience psychological disturbance. When it is for better, they can focus on the same event and initially explicitly rehearse the flexible and/or non-extreme attitude that they are striving to hold about the same adversity (Ellis & Joffe Ellis, 2011). Here is a set of instructions to help the client use imagery rehearsal of flexible and/or non-extreme attitudes. Remember that the client can use this method about a past, present or future adversity.

- Imagine yourself in the situation in which you disturbed yourself.
- Focus on the adversity in this situation. This will be the aspect of the situation that you were most disturbed about.
- Allow yourself to experience briefly the disturbed feeling.

- Use this feeling as a cue to rehearse the flexible and/or non-extreme attitude that you are striving to develop and hold this attitude in place until you have experienced a change of emotion from unhealthy negative to healthy negative.
- Practise doing this for ten minutes at least three times a day.

BACK TO FRANK

Frank used this method daily and whenever else he began to feel unhealthily angry about the unfairness of being passed over.

- Frank remembered how he found out that he had been passed over for promotion.
- He focused on how unfairly he had been treated.
- He allowed himself to experience the unhealthy anger he felt about this adversity briefly.
- He then used this feeling as a cue to rehearse the following flexible: "I would have preferred to have been treated fairly, but sadly and regretfully, there is no reason why this absolutely should not have happened". He held this attitude in place until he experienced a change of emotion from unhealthy anger to healthy anger.
- He practised doing this for ten minutes at least three times a day.

This method helped Frank to increase his conviction in this flexible attitude which in turn helped him to maintain his healthy anger in the face of unfairness in this and other contexts.

Understand the change process

It may be useful for the client to understand a number of points about the process of change that they have embarked upon (Dryden & Neenan, 2004a). Most clients will benefit from this discussion once they have gained intellectual insight and are about to embark on a process designed to promote emotional insight. However, please note that some clients may prefer to have this information at the outset. Thus, there is no ideal time for this topic to be covered in therapy as it will vary from client to client. Such points, whenever they are covered in the therapeutic process are meant to sustain the client when the going gets rough.

EXPECT THAT THE FIRST RESPONSE TO AN ADVERSITY WILL BE PROBLEMATIC AND RESPOND TO IT IN HEALTHY WAYS

Often clients get discouraged during the process of working to change their attitudes from rigid and/or extreme to flexible and/or non-extreme.

Once they have gained experience of questioning both sets of attitudes and strengthening their healthy flexible and non-extreme attitudes, they expect that after a while their first response to an adversity will be healthy, and when it is not, they think that they have made no progress and they give up the process of change.

Thus, it is vital for the client to understand that when they encounter adversity, no matter how much they have practised thinking healthily (i.e. flexibly and in a non-extreme way) about it previously, their first response to that adversity may well still be unhealthy (i.e. rigid and extreme). This initial response is typical, and the important thing is that the client realises this and that they respond quickly to this initial unhealthy thinking in ways that they have previously learned and practised. This is why I say that in the face of adversity the client's response to their first response to the adversity is important. If the client initially responds unhealthily to the adversity but responds to that response in a healthy manner, then they will continue the process of change. However, if they get discouraged by their first response and do nothing, then this will obstruct the change process.

ATTITUDE DISSONANCE

When the client is trying to change their attitude, it is likely that they will experience dissonance between the rigid attitude that they wish to change and the flexible attitude that they wish to develop. Clients often say at the beginning of the attitude change process that while they know that their flexible attitude is true, logical and helpful and that their rigid attitude is false, illogical and unconstructive, they still have conviction in the latter and not in the former. Thus, clients say of their flexible attitude things like, "I believe it in my head, but not in my gut". This phenomenon which I call 'attitude dissonance' is very common, and if the client accepts it as such it should not prove an obstacle to change. Such dissonance will disappear once the client has done the requisite amount of attitude change practice. The best way of dispelling such dissonance is for the client to keep their flexible attitude and related behaviour, imagery, talk and thinking in harmony and to do so over time (Dryden & Neenan, 2004b).

FEELINGS ARE OFTEN THE LAST TO CHANGE

Clients often become discouraged when their feelings don't change after they have questioned their rigid attitudes and acted on their alternative flexible attitudes. Consequently, they give up trying to change their attitudes. It is important to recognise that feelings are the last to change and when they do, it is an indication that the client's new flexible attitudes are beginning to take root. If the client understands this phenomenon, then they will persist with acting and thinking in ways that support their developing flexible attitudes.

THE PRACTICE PRINCIPLE: IT'S LIKE GOING TO THE GYM

Changing an attitude is a bit like going to the gym. If the client wants to get fit and stay fit, then they need to go to the gym regularly and spend some time there doing the required exercises. However, it is important that the client does not overdo it in the gym. 'Little and often' is better than 'a lot and seldom'. Exactly the same is true when it comes to the client changing their attitude. Such regular practice can be in the situation when facing an adversity, using imagery while imagining facing the adversity or both (Dryden & Neenan, 2004c).

Helping the client to deal with the thinking consequences of rigid / extreme attitudes

As I pointed out in Part 1 of this concise guide, when the client holds a rigid/extreme attitude towards an adversity, then they tend to make inferences about relevant aspects of the adversity that are highly distorted and skewed to the negative. These are regarded as thinking consequences (TCs) of rigid/extreme attitudes. In this section, I will discuss a number of ways to help client not get caught up with these thoughts and to focus on changing the rigid/extrme attitudes that spawn them. There are three ways that a client can deal with these TCs (Dryden, 2015).

THE CLIENT CAN USE THE TCS TO IDENTIFY AND RESPOND TO THEIR RIGID/EXTREME ATTITUDE AND THEN DEVELOP AND REHEARSE THE FLEXIBLE/NON-EXTREME ATTITUDE ALTERNATIVE

If the client has not yet identified their rigid/extreme attitude, they can use their thinking consequence to identify and question it. If they *have* identified the adversity about which they have disturbed themself, but have not identified the rigid/extreme attitude, then they can do so by using their TCs to ask themself the question, for example: "What demand am I making about this adversity that has led to these TCs?" Once discovered, then the client can respond to this rigid attitude as discussed above and rehearse and develop their new flexible/non-extreme attitude deliberately focusing on the consequent realistic and balanced TCs of this new attitude if they need to do so.

Back to Frank Using this approach, Frank would focus on his highly distorted, negatively skewed thinking consequence of his rigid attitude about the adversity of being treated unfairly (i.e. 'Life is unfair') and ask himself: "What demand am I making about being treated unfairly that has led me to think that life is unfair?" The answer in Frank's case was, "I absolutely should not have been treated unfairly". Once he has identified this attitude he would respond to it as previously shown and rehearse and devclop his flexible/non-extreme attitude (namely, "I would have preferred to have been treated fairly, but sadly and regretfully, there is no reason why this absolutely should have happened") while focusing on the consequent realistic and balanced TCs of this new attitude (i.e. "Not being promoted may be unfair, but life as a whole can be fair and unfair").

By contrast, if the client has *not* identified the adversity about which they have disturbed themself (i.e. they do not know what their 'A' is), then they first need to do so. See Table 2.6 for an example of how a client can do this (in this case, Frank). Once the client has identified the adversity, they can proceed as above.

THE CLIENT CAN RESPOND TO THESE TCS AND THEN RETURN TO THE RIGID/EXTREME ATTITUDE THAT SPAWNED THEM AND RESPOND TO IT

Sometimes the existence of highly distorted, negatively skewed thinking consequences of rigid/extreme makes it difficult for the client to identify and/or respond to their rigid/extreme attitude. In this case, the client may gain benefit by first responding to these TCs first before turning their attention to responding to their rigid/extreme attitude.

Responding to a highly distorted and negatively skewed TC of a rigid/extreme attitude involves the client standing back and asking themself one or more questions until they have developed a realistic alternative to this TC as demonstrated by Frank.

Back to Frank Here is how Frank would have used such questioning:

- *How likely is it that my TC (that life is unfair) is true*?

  Answer: "Not true at all. Life has unfair aspects, but it also has fair aspects".

- *Would an objective jury agree that my TC (that life is unfair) is true? If not, what would the jury's verdict be?*

  Answer: "The jury's verdict would be that this statement is definitely false. Rather 'life' can be said to be a mixture of fairness and unfairness and a whole host of events that be placed outside the 'fairness/unfairness' framework."

Table 2.6 Windy's magic question (WMQ) with Frank

The purpose of this questioning technique is for the client to be helped or to help themself to identify the adversity or 'A' as quickly as possible (i.e. what the client is most disturbed about) once their unhealthy negative emotion at 'C' has been assessed, and the 'situation' in which 'C' has occurred has been identified and briefly described. Here, I will show how I used this method with Frank.
Step 1: I asked Frank to focus on his disturbed emotional 'C' (here, 'unhealthy anger').
Step 2: I then asked him to focus on the situation in which 'C' occurred (here 'being passed over for promotion').
Step 3: Next, I asked Frank: *"Which ingredient could I give you to eliminate or significantly reduce 'C'?"* (here, unhealthy anger). (In this case, Frank said "'being shown that I was not being treated unfairly"). At this point, I took care that Frank did not change the situation (i.e. he did not say something like "getting the promotion").
Step 4: The opposite is probably Frank's adversity or 'A' (i.e. 'being treated unfairly'), but I checked to see if this was the case. I asked: *"So when you were passed over for promotion, were you most unhealthily angry about being treated unfairly?"* If not, I would use the question again until Frank confirmed what he was most unhealthily angry about in the described situation.

- *Did I view (am I viewing) the situation realistically? If not, how could I have viewed (can I view) it more realistically?*

  Answer: "I am viewing this most unrealistically. It is much more realistic to say that life is too complex to be given a single rating and while it may have been unfair for me not to be promoted such unfairness does not define life but can be incorporated a view of life where unfairness and fairness happen".

- *If a friend had told me that they had faced the same situation as I faced and had made the same conclusion, what would I say to him / her about the validity of their conclusion and why? How would I encourage the person to view the situation instead?*

  Answer: "If a friend had been unfairly denied promotion, I would understand why they might conclude that life was unfair and would communicate my understanding to them. However, I would then gently point out that they were overgeneralising from one aspect of life to the whole of life and encourage them not to do so".

THE CLIENT CAN ACKNOWLEDGE THE EXISTENCE OF THE TCS, BUT NOT ENGAGE WITH THEM

Even if the client uses both the methods outlined above, they may still find that their highly distorted TCs come to and remain in their mind. This is perfectly natural for two main reasons. First, the client has probably had more experience thinking the TCs of a rigid/extreme attitude than the realistic and balanced TCs of a flexible/non-extreme attitude. Second, emotionally-charged TCs of a rigid/extreme attitude take quite a long time to fade from the client's mind even if they do not engage with them. If the client engages with them after using the two approaches to TCs outlined above they will more likely keep them in mind rather than if they did not engage with them.

Why might a client continually engage with these TCs? The major reason is that they may wish to get rid of these thoughts and think that continually engaging with the thoughts will lead them to be thoroughly convinced that they are not realistic and that this thorough conviction will get rid of them. The client here is wrong on two counts. First, it is not likely that the client will become thoroughly convinced that highly distorted TCs are false in a short period of time. Rather, the client needs to increase their conviction in the falseness of the TCs bit by bit in small, time-limited chunks. Second, if the client tries to get rid of thoughts, then they will only succeed in keeping them alive. There is a famous psychological experiment that shows that if a person is asked to think of a white polar bear and then instruct themself to dismiss this thought from their mind, then the person will, in fact, keep this thought in their mind (Wegner, 1994).

But how can a client acknowledge but not engage with highly distorted and negatively skewed TCs? Let me show how by first outlining what I mean by 'acknowledgment of TCs'. By this, I mean that the client notices the existence of these thoughts and recognises that they are highly distorted, negatively skewed TCs of their rigid/extreme attitude. They accept but do not like the fact that these thoughts are in their mind and that they will stay in their mind until they are not in their mind.

Now, let me consider what I mean by non-engagement with TCs. This can best be understood by first understanding what it means to engage with them. There are two forms of engagement with such TCs: deliberate engagement and unwitting engagement.

- In deliberate engagement with TCs, the client actively thinks about the thought and how to prevent it from becoming reality, for example. Thus, if a client's TC is "Everyone will laugh at me if I make a mistake", engaging with this thought involves the client thinking, for example: a) what they can do to prevent themself from making a mistake; and b) how to respond when people are laughing at one.

- In unwitting engagement with TCs, the client is actively trying *not* to engage with the thought. Paradoxically, this has the effect that they are, in fact, engaging with it, but are not wishing to do so. Thus, if the client decides to watch TV in order to distract themself from their TCs, then they will generally fail to do so since, as we have seen above, the more a person tries not to think about something, the more they will tend to think about it. Indeed in unwitting engagement, the client is engaged with thinking about what they can do so that they don't think about their TCs!

Non-engagement with highly distorted and negatively skewed TCs of a rigid/extreme attitude involves the client getting on with life as they would do if these thoughts were not in their mind. Thus, if the client were planning to watch a TV programme, then they should do so even though the TCs may still be in their mind. This is different from the above in that the client is not trying to distract themself from their TCs. Here, the client acknowledges the fact that these thoughts may be in their mind (see previous section), but they get on with whatever they have decided to get on with regardless of their presence (or absence). As the client does so, they should accept, but not like that their enjoyment or concentration may be impaired to some degree by the presence of these thoughts.

Clients report that the effect of such acknowledgement and non-engagement is that their TCs are less present in their mind than when they engage with them or try to get rid of them.

Here are two useful analogies that clients have found helpful when practising non-engaged acknowledgment of highly distorted, negatively skewed TCs.

- **The radio analogy**

"When you have very distorted thoughts, be aware that they are stemming from your rigid/extreme attitude, so think of them as voices that are on the radio. You can actively listen to them or not listen to them. The second involves accepting them, but not liking them being there, but if you get on with stuff, then you will soon forget that they are there. As soon as you are aware that they are not there though, they may come back. But when this happens, just accept this and get on with stuff even though the radio is on".

- **The light bulb analogy**

"Imagine that you stare at a lit light bulb and then close your eyes. What happens? You will still have an image of the light bulb on your retina which will take a while to fade. If you accept that this is natural and go about your business, you will eventually note that the image of the light bulb has gone. However, if you keep returning to gaze at the light bulb, you will re-stimulate the retina with its image, thus keeping it alive longer on your retina. The same is the case with your very distorted thoughts. Understand that they stem from your rigid/extreme attitude and that they will stay in your mind for a while even after you have developed the alternative flexible/non-extreme attitude. Then, recognise that the best way for these thoughts to fade is for you to go on with your business without engaging with them. Re-engaging with them will only serve to re-stimulate your mind with their presence".

This discussion of how to deal with the highly distorted, negatively skewed thinking consequences of rigid/extreme attitudes brings this concise guide to a close. I hope you have found it helpful and if so, I have provided a number of suggestions for further reading below.

In addition, if you have any feedback for me you can send it to windy@windydryden.com.

Notes

1 In Appendix 3, I will outline arguments that can be used to help clients think about these issues clearly.

2 In this chapter, I will focus on the situation where the client works to change their rigid attitudes to flexible ones since, as we saw in Part 1 of this concise guide, these are at the very core of a disturbed and healthy response to adversity respectively. The client can apply the same methods to any of their extreme attitudes to help them to change these extreme attitudes to non-extreme ones.

Appendix 1
A guide to the eight emotional problems and their healthy alternatives with adversities, basic attitudes and associated behaviour and thinking

Anxiety vs Concern

Adversity	• *The client is facing a threat to their personal domain.*	
Basic attitude	**RIGID AND EXTREME**	**FLEXIBLE AND NON-EXTREME**
Emotion	**Anxiety**	**Concern**
Behaviour	• The client avoids the threat. • The client withdraws physically from the threat. • The client wards off the threat (e.g. by rituals or superstitious behaviour). • The client tries to neutralise the threat (e.g. by being nice to people of whom they afraid). • The client distracts themself from the threat by engaging in other activity. • The client keeps checking on the current status of the threat hoping to find that it has disappeared or become benign. • The client seeks reassurance from others that the threat is benign.	• The client faces up to the threat without using any safety-seeking measures. • The client takes constructive action to deal with the threat. • The client seeks support from others to help them face up to the threat and then takes constructive action by themself rather than rely on the other people to handle it for them or to be there to rescue them. • The client prepares to meet the threat but do not over-prepare.

	• The client seeks support from others so that if the threat happens these others will handle it or be there to rescue the client. • The client over-prepares in order to minimise the threat happening or so that they are prepared to meet it (NB it is the over-preparation that is the problem here). • The client tranquillises their feelings so that they don't think about the threat. • The client overcompensates for feeling vulnerable by seeking out an even greater threat to prove to themself that they can cope.	
Subsequent thinking	*Threat-exaggerated thinking*	
	• The client overestimates the probability of the threat occurring.	• The client is realistic about the probability of the threat occurring.
	• The client underestimates their ability to cope with the threat.	• The client views the threat realistically.
	• The client ruminates about the threat.	• The client realistically appraises their ability to cope with the threat.
	• The client creates an even more negative threat in their mind.	• The client thinks about what to do concerning dealing with the threat constructively rather than ruminate about it.
	• The client magnifies the negative consequences of the threat and minimises its positive consequences.	• The client has more task-relevant thoughts than in anxiety.
	• The client has more task-irrelevant thoughts than in concern.	• The client pictures themself dealing with the threat in a realistic way.

	Safety-seeking thinking • The client withdraws mentally from the threat. • The client tries to persuade themself that the threat is not imminent and that they are 'imagining' it. • The client thinks in ways designed to reassure themself that the threat is benign or if not, that its consequences will be insignificant. • The client distracts themself from the threat e.g. by focusing on mental scenes of safety and well-being. • The client over-prepares mentally in order to minimise the threat happening or so that they are prepared to meet it (NB once again it is the over-preparation that is the problem here). • The client pictures themself dealing with the threat in a masterful way. • The client overcompensates for feeling vulnerable by picturing themself dealing effectively with an even bigger threat.	

Depression vs Sadness

Adversity	• *The client has experienced a loss from the sociotropic and / or autonomous realms of their personal domain.* • *The client has experienced failure within the sociotropic and / or autonomous realms of their personal domain.* • *The client or others have experienced an undeserved plight.*	
Basic attitude	**RIGID AND EXTREME**	**FLEXIBLE AND NON-EXTREME**
Emotion	**Depression**	**Sadness**
Behaviour	• The client becomes overly dependent on and seeks to cling to others (particularly in sociotropic depression). • The client bemoans their fate or that of others to anyone who will listen (particularly in pity-based depression). • The client creates an environment consistent with their depressed feelings. • The client attempts to terminate feelings of depression in self-destructive ways. • The client either pushes away attempts to comfort them (in autonomous depression) or uses such comfort to reinforce their dependency (in sociotropic depression) or their self- or other-pity (in pity-based depression).	• The client seeks out reinforcements after a period of mourning (particularly when their inferential theme is loss). • The client creates an environment inconsistent with depressed feelings and consistent with feelings of sadness. • The client expresses their feelings of sadness about the loss, failure or undeserved plight and talks in a non-complaining way about these feelings to significant others. • The client allows themself to be comforted in a way that helps them to express their feelings of sadness and mourn their loss.

Subsequent thinking	• The client sees only negative aspects of the loss, failure or undeserved plight. • The client thinks of other losses, failures and undeserved plights that they (and in the case of the latter, others) have experienced. • The client thinks they are unable to help themself (helplessness). • The client only sees pain and blackness in the future (hopelessness). • The client sees themself being totally dependent on others (in autonomous depression). • The client sees themself as being disconnected from others (in sociotropic depression). • The client sees the world as full of undeservedness and unfairness (in plight-based depression). • The client tends to ruminate concerning the source of their depression and its consequences.	• The client is able to recognise both negative and positive aspects of the loss or failure. • The client thinks they are able to help themself. • The client looks to the future with hope.

Guilt vs Remorse

Adversity	• *The client has broken their moral code.* • *The client has failed to live up to their moral code.* • *The client has hurt someone's feelings.*	
Basic attitude	**RIGID AND EXTREME**	**FLEXIBLE AND NON-EXTREME**
Emotion	**Guilt**	**Remorse**
Behaviour	• The client escapes from the unhealthy pain of guilt in self-defeating ways. • The client begs forgiveness from the person they have wronged. • The client promises unrealistically that they will not 'sin' again. • The client punishes themself physically or by deprivation. • The client defensively disclaims responsibility for wrongdoing. • The client makes excuses for their behaviour. • The client rejects offers of forgiveness.	• The client faces up to the healthy pain that accompanies the realisation that they have sinned. • The client asks, but does not beg, for forgiveness. • The client understands the reasons for their wrongdoing and acts on their understanding. • The client atones for the sin by taking a penalty. • The client makes appropriate amends. • The client does not make excuses for their behaviour or enact other defensive behaviour. • The client accepts offers for forgiveness.
Subsequent thinking	• The client concluds that they have definitely committed the sin. • The client assumes more personal responsibility than the situation warrants.	• The client takes into account all relevant data when judging whether or not they have 'sinned'.

	• The client assigns far less responsibility to others than is warranted. • The client dismisses possible mitigating factors for their behaviour. • The client only sees their behaviour in a guilt-related context and fails to put it into an overall context. • The client thinks that they will receive retribution.	• The client assumes an appropriate level of personal responsibility. • The client assigns an appropriate level of responsibility to others. • The client takes into account mitigating factors. • The client puts their behaviour into overall context. • The client thinks they may be penalised rather than receive retribution.

Shame vs Disappointment

Adversity	• *Something highly negative has been revealed about the client (or about a group with whom the client identify) by themselves or by others.* • *The client has acted in a way that falls very short of their ideal.* • *Others look down on or shun the client (or a group with whom the client identifies) or the client thinks that they do.*	
Basic attitude	**RIGID AND EXTREME**	**FLEXIBLE AND NON-EXTREME**
Emotion	**Shame**	**Disappointment**
Behaviour	• The client removes themself from the 'gaze' of others. • The client isolates themself from others. • The client saves face by attacking other(s) who have 'shamed' them. • The client defends their threatened self-esteem in self-defeating ways. • The client ignores attempts by others to restore social equilibrium.	• The client continues to participate actively in social interaction. • The client responds positively to attempts of others to restore social equilibrium.
Subsequent thinking	• The client overestimates the negativity of the information revealed. • The client overestimates the likelihood that the judging group will notice or be interested in the information. • The client overestimates the degree of disapproval they (or their reference group) will receive. • The client overestimates how long any disapproval will last.	• The client sees the information revealed in a compassionate self-accepting context. • The client is realistic about the likelihood that the judging group will notice or be interested in the information revealed. • The client is realistic about the degree of disapproval they (or their reference group) will receive. • The client is realistic about how long any disapproval will last.

Hurt vs Sorrow

Adversity	• *Others treat the client badly (and the client thinks they do not deserve such treatment).* • *The client thinks that the other person has devalued their relationship (i.e. someone indicates that their relationship with the client is less important to them than the relationship is to the client).*	
Basic attitude	**RIGID AND EXTREME**	**FLEXIBLE AND NON-EXTREME**
Emotion	**Hurt**	**Sorrow**
Behaviour	• The client stops communicating with the other person. • The client sulks and makes obvious that they feel hurt without disclosing details of the matter. • The client indirectly criticises or punishes the other person for their offence. • The client tells others how badly they have been treated, but doesn't take any responsibility for any contribution they may have made to this.	• The client communicates their feelings to the other directly. • The client requests that the other person acts in a fairer manner towards them. • The client discusses the situation with others in a balanced way, focusing on the way they have been treated and taking responsibility for any contribution they may have made to this.
Subsequent thinking	• The client overestimates the unfairness of the other person's behaviour. • The client thinks that the other person does not care for them or is indifferent to them.	• The client is realistic about the degree of unfairness in the other person's behaviour. • The client thinks that the other person has acted badly rather than demonstrating lack of caring or indifference.

	• The client sees themself as alone, uncared for or misunderstood. • The client tends to think of past 'hurts'. • The client thinks that the other person has to make the first move to them and dismisses the possibility of making the first move towards that person.	• The client sees themself as being in a poor situation, but still connected to, cared for by and understood by others not directly involved in the situation. • If the client thinks of past hurts they do so with less frequency and less intensity than when they feel hurt. • The client is open to the idea of making the first move towards the other person.

Unhealthy Anger vs Healthy Anger

Adversity	• *The client thinks that they have been frustrated in some way or their movement towards an important goal has been obstructed.* • *Someone has treated the client badly.* • *Someone has transgressed one of the client's personal rules.* • *The client has transgressed one of their own personal rules.* • *Someone or something has threatened the client's self-esteem or disrespected them.*	
Basic attitude	**RIGID AND EXTREME**	**FLEXIBLE AND NON-EXTREME**
Emotion	**Unhealthy anger**	**Healthy anger**
Behaviour	• The client attacks the other(s) physically. • The client attacks the other(s) verbally. • The client attacks the other(s) passive-aggressively. • The client displaces the attack on to another person, animal or object. • The client withdraws aggressively. • The client recruits allies against the other(s).	• The client asserts themself with the other(s). • The client requests, but does not demand, behavioural change from the other(s). • The client leaves an unsatisfactory situation non-aggressively after taking steps to deal with it.
Subsequent thinking	• The client overestimates the extent to which the other(s) acted deliberately. • The client sees malicious intent in the motives of the other(s). • The client sees themself as definitely right and the other(s) as definitely wrong.	• The client thinks that the other(s) may have acted deliberately, but they also recognise that this may not have been the case. • The client is able to see the point of view of the other(s).

	• The client is unable to see the point of view of the other(s). • The client plots to exact revenge. • The client ruminates about the other's behaviour and imagines coming out on top.	• The client has fleeting, rather than sustained thoughts to exact revenge. • The client thinks that other(s) may have had malicious intent in their motives, but they also recognise that this may not have been the case. • The client thinks that they are probably rather than definitely right and the other(s) as probably rather than definitely wrong.

Unhealthy Jealousy vs Healthy Jealousy (or Relationship Concern)

Adversity	• *A threat is posed to the client's relationship with their partner from a third person.* • *A threat is posed by uncertainty faced by the client concerning their partner's whereabouts, behaviour or thinking in the context of the first threat.*	
Basic attitude	**RIGID AND EXTREME**	**FLEXIBLE AND NON-EXTREME**
Emotion	**Unhealthy jealousy**	**Healthy jealousy (relationship concern)**
Behaviour	• The client seeks constant reassurance from their partner that they are loved. • The client monitors the actions and feelings of their partner. • The client searches for evidence that their partner is involved with someone else. • The client attempts to restrict the movements or activities of their partner. • The client sets tests which their partner has to pass. • The client retaliates for their partner's presumed infidelity. • The client sulks.	• The client allows their partner to initiate expressing love for them without prompting them or seeking reassurance once they have done so. • The client allows their partner freedom without monitoring his/her feelings, actions and whereabouts. • The client allows their partner to show natural interest in members of the opposite sex without setting tests. • The client communicates their concern for their relationship in an open and non-blaming manner.

Subsequent thinking	• The client exaggerates any threat to their relationship that does exist. • The client thinks the loss of their relationship is imminent. • The client misconstrues their partner's ordinary conversations with relevant others as having romantic or sexual connotations. • The client constructs visual images of their partner's infidelity. • If their partner admits to finding another person attractive, the client thinks that their partner finds that person more attractive than the client and that s/he will leave the client for this other person.	• The client tend not to exaggerate any threat to their relationship that does exist. • The client does not misconstrue ordinary conversations between their partner and another men/women. • The client does not construct visual images of their partner's infidelity. • The client accepts that their partner will find others attractive but the client does not inevitably see this as a threat.

Unhealthy Envy vs Healthy Envy

Adversity	• *Another person possesses and enjoys something desirable that the client does not have.*	
Basic attitude	**RIGID AND EXTREME**	**FLEXIBLE AND NON-EXTREME**
Emotion	**Unhealthy envy**	**Healthy envy**
Behaviour	• The client verbally disparages the person who has the desired possession to others. • The client verbally disparages the desired possession to others. • If the client had the chance, they would take away the desired possession from the other (either so that the client would have it or that the other is deprived of it). • If the client had the chance, they would spoil or destroy the desired possession so that the other person does not have it.	• The client strives to obtain the desired possession if it is truly what they want.
Subsequent thinking	• The client tends to denigrate in their mind the value of the desired possession and/or the person who possesses it.	• The client honestly admits to themself that they do indeed want the desired possession if this is the case.

	• The client tries to convince themself that they are happy with their possessions (although they are not). • The client thinks about how to acquire the desired possession regardless of its usefulness. • The client thinks about how to deprive the other person of the desired possession. • The client thinks about how to spoil or destroy the other's desired possession. • The client thinks about all the other things the other has that they don't have.	• The client is honest with themself if they are not happy with their possessions, rather than defensively trying to convince themself that they are happy with them when they are not. • The client thinks about how to obtain the desired possession because they desire it for healthy reasons. • The client can allow the other person to have and enjoy the desired possession without denigrating that person or the possession. • The client does not think about how to spoil or destroy the other's desired possession. • The client thinks about what the other has and lacks and what they have and lack.

Appendix 2
A list of inferential (cognitive) distortions, their realistic and balanced alternatives, descriptions and examples

Inferential distortion and its realistic and balanced alternative	Description	Example
All-or-nothing thinking	The client sees things in black or white terms, without any shades of grey.	• "Either I will do very well or I will fail."
Continuum thinking	The client sees things along a continuum.	• "If I don't do very well, I may do well or quite well."
Always thinking	The client focuses on a negative event and thinks that it will always keep happening.	• "Now that my boss has criticised me he will always keep on doing so."
Realistic anti-always thinking	The client focuses on a negative event and thinks that while it might happen again, it is also possible that it may not. There is no evidence that it will always keep happening.	• "There is no evidence that my boss will always keep criticising just because he has just done so. He may, but it is more probable that he won't."

Inferential distortion and its realistic and balanced alternative	**Description**	**Example**
Never thinking Realistic anti-never thinking	The client focuses on a possible positive event and thinks that it will never happen. The client focuses on a possible positive event and acknowledges the possibility that it may happen.	• "My colleague has just been commended for her good work, but this will never happen to me." • "My colleague has just been commended for her good work and if I do good work, then this could happen to me."
Mental filter Balanced filter	The client dwells on the negatives and ignores the positives. The client acknowledges both the positives and the negatives.	• "Even though most people seemed to like my presentation, I can only think of the one or two people who looked bored during it." • "Most people seemed to like my presentation and although one or two looked bored, I can't expect everyone to show interest."
Discounting the positives Affirming the positives	The client strips the positive out of something positive happening to them. The client fully acknowledges the positives that happen to them and allows themself to be nourished by the experiences.	• "While it is true that a lot of people said they liked my talk, they only said that to be kind." • "A lot of people said they liked my talk and I am going to really process that."

Inferential distortion and its realistic and balanced alternative	Description	Example
Mind reading	The client thinks that they know what others are thinking in the absence of evidence that this is the case.	• "My boss was thinking that I am not up to the job."
Seeking clarification	The client seeks clarification about what others are thinking by asking them.	• "I think that my boss was thinking that I am not up to the job, but I really don't know. I will ask him."
Fortune telling	The client makes predictions about the future in the absence of evidence.	• "My boss will not recommend me for promotion at the next round."
Living in the present	The client may make predictions but tests them against the available evidence and concentrates on what is going on now.	• "I think that my boss will not recommend me for promotion, but as I don't have any evidence for that I am going to concentrate on making it very difficult for him not to recommend me."
Magnification	The client blows things out of proportion with respect to bad things happening to them and their negative qualities.	• "If I don't give a good presentation then I will be stuck at this level for years."
Keeping things in proportion	The client keeps the bad things that happen to them and their negative qualities in reasonable proportion.	• "If I don't give a good presentation, I can learn to improve and still raise my work level in the future if I do."

Inferential distortion and its realistic and balanced alternative	Description	Example
Minimisation	The client minimises the importance of good things in their life or their positive qualities.	• "If I passed, then anyone can do so. It's no big deal."
Appreciating the importance of the positive	The client acknowledges the importance of good things in their life or their positive qualities.	• "If I passed then that is an achievement regardless of what anyone lese did."
Emotional reasoning	The client assumes that their feelings reflect reality.	• "I feel anxious so something bad is about to happen to me."
Checking one's emotional intuition	The client does not automatically assume that their feelings reflect reality. They check them against the available evidence.	• "I feel anxious, but that does not mean that something bad is about to happen to me. It means that I think that it is."
Cognitive reasoning	The client assumes that their thoughts reflect reality.	• "I think that my colleague doesn't want to work with me so it is true that he doesn't."
Checking one's thinking	The client does not automatically assume that their thoughts reflect reality. They check them against the available evidence.	• "I think that my colleague doesn't want to work with me, but I need to check this out."

Inferential distortion and its realistic and balanced alternative	Description	Example
Labelling	The client focuses on their behaviour and that of others and labels the person with that behaviour.	• "My colleague betrayed my trust and thus, she is an untrustworthy person."
Aspect focus without labelling	The client focuses on their behaviour and that of others, but refrains from labelling the person with that behaviour.	• "My colleague betrayed my trust, but it does not make her an untrustworthy person. I may be able to trust her in the future over certain things, but not over others."
Personalisation	The client assumes that an event must relate to them.	• "My team were not successful with the bid which proves it was my fault."
Realistic attributions	The client does not automatically assume that an event must relate to them. They are open to the possibility that it may or may not do so and will test these assumptions against the available evidence.	• "My team were not successful with the bid to which we may all have contributed some responsibility. I need to assess this in an open way with my team."

Appendix 3
Arguments to help clients examine their rigid/extreme and flexible/non-extreme attitudes

	Rigid/extreme attitudes	Flexible/non-extreme attitudes
Rigid attitudes vs flexible attitudes	• Help the client see that when they hold a rigid attitude, they dogmatically attempt to make the world fit their preference. Encourage them to see that this rigid attitude obstructs them from seeing the world as it is and leads them to hold on to their demanded version of the world. Thus, a rigid attitude is inconsistent with reality.	• Help the client to see that when they hold a flexible attitude, they acknowledge what they want and try to get it but accept that this does not have to happen. They do not demand that their preferences are met. This helps them to see the world as it is rather than as they want it to be. Thus, a flexible attitude is consistent with reality.
	• Help the client to see that when they hold a rigid attitude, they attempt to extract an 'ought' from a 'preference' which is illogical. This a rigid attitude is illogical.	• Help the client to see that when they hold a flexible attitude, this helps them to see that there is no logical connection between an 'ought' and a 'preference'. Therefore, a flexible attitude is logical.

	Rigid/extreme attitudes	Flexible/non-extreme attitudes
	• Have the client focus on the emotional, behavioural and thinking consequences of their rigid attitude and encourage them to see that these consequences are unhelpful and unconstructive to them in the long term.	• Have the client focus on the emotional, behavioural and thinking consequences of their flexible attitude and encourage them to see that these consequences are helpful and constructive to them in the long term.
Awfulising attitudes vs non-awfulising attitudes	• Help the client see that when they hold an awfulising towards an adversity, they think that: i) nothing could be worse; ii) the adversity in question is worse than 100% bad; iii) no good could possibly come from this adversity which is wholly bad; and iv) the adversity cannot be transcended. Therefore, an awfulising attitude is inconsistent with reality.	• Help the client to see that when they hold a non-awfulising attitude towards an adversity, they acknowledge that: i) things can be worse for them; ii) the adversity is thus not 100% bad; iii) they can learn something productive from the adversity, and thus good can come from the adversity; and iv) the adversity can be transcended. No matter how bad it is, it is possible for them to process it and move on with life. Therefore, a non-awfulising attitude is consistent with reality.
	• Help the client to see that an awfulising attitude has two components: i) "It is bad that the adversity has happened" (non-extreme); and ii) "… and therefore it is awful" (extreme). Show the client that it is illogical to try and derive something extreme from what is non-extreme and therefore an	• Help the client to see that a non-awfulising attitude has two components: i) "It is bad that the adversity has happened" (non-extreme); and ii) "but it is not awful that it occurred" (non-extreme). Show the client that as both parts of this attitude

	Rigid/extreme attitudes	Flexible/non-extreme attitudes
	awfulising attitude is illogical. • Have the client focus on the emotional, behavioural and thinking consequences of their awfulising attitude and encourage them to see that these consequences are unhelpful and unconstructive to them in the long term.	are non-extreme, we can say that a non-awfulising attitude is logical since it attempts to derive something non-extreme from something that is also non-extreme. • Have the client focus on the emotional, behavioural and thinking consequences of their non-awfulising attitude and encourage them to see that these consequences are helpful and constructive to them in the long term.
Discomfort intolerance attitudes vs discomfort tolerance attitudes	• Help the client to see that when they hold a discomfort intolerance attitude towards an adversity, they contend *at the time* the idea that they will die or disintegrate if the discomfort or frustration continues to exist or that they will lose the capacity to experience happiness if the discomfort or frustration continues to exist. Both of these contentions are untrue and therefore a discomfort intolerance attitude is inconsistent with reality.	• Help the client to see that when they hold a discomfort tolerance attitude towards an adversity they acknowledge that: i) it is hard for them to tolerate it; ii) they can do so; iii) the adversity is worth bearing and assuming this; iv) they are willing to do so; and v) they commit to doing so. As all of these components are true, a discomfort tolerance attitude is consistent with reality.

	Rigid/extreme attitudes	Flexible/non-extreme attitudes
	• Help the client to see that a discomfort intolerance attitude has two components: i) "It is hard to tolerate the existence of the adversity" (non-extreme); and ii) "… and therefore I can't bear it if it exists" (extreme). Show the client that it is illogical to try and derive something extreme from what is non-extreme and therefore a discomfort intolerance attitude is illogical. • Have the client focus on the emotional, behavioural and thinking consequences of their discomfort intolerance attitude and encourage them to see that these consequences are unhelpful and unconstructive to them in the long term.	• Help the client to see that all five of the above components are non-extreme and are logically linked together by being non-extreme. Given this, a discomfort tolerance attitude is logical. • Have the client focus on the emotional, behavioural and thinking consequences of their discomfort tolerance attitude and encourage them to see that these consequences are helpful and constructive to them in the long term.
Devaluation attitudes vs acceptance attitudes	• Help the client to see that when they hold a devaluation attitude towards an adversity they contend that: i) a person (self or other) can legitimately be given a single global rating that defines their essence and the worth of a person is dependent upon conditions that change (e.g. my worth goes up when I do well and goes down when I don't do well); and/or ii) the world can legitimately be given a single rating that defines	• Help the client to see that when they hold an acceptance attitude towards an adversity they contend that: i) a person (self or other) cannot be legitimately be given a single global rating that defines their essence and the worth of a person is fixed and is not dependent upon conditions that change; and/or ii) the world cannot legitimately be given a single rating that defines its essential nature and that the value

	Rigid/extreme attitudes	Flexible/non-extreme attitudes
	its essential nature and that the value of the world varies according to what happens within it (e.g. the value of the world goes up when something fair occurs and goes down when something unfair happens). Also, help the client to see that when they hold a devaluation attitude towards an adversity, they further contend that: iii) a person can be rated on the basis of one of his or her aspects; and iv) the world can be rated on the basis of one of its aspects. All these contentions are false and therefore a devaluation attitude is inconsistent with reality. • Help the client to see that a devaluation attitude has two components: i) an 'aspect evaluation' component which acknowledges that it is possible and realistic to evaluate a *part* of a person or what has happened to that person; and ii) an 'asserted devaluation' component which claims that one can rate negatively the *whole* of a person or the world. Attempts to rate the whole on the basis of a part is illogical and is	of the world is fixed and does not vary according to what happens within it. Also help the client to see that when they hold an acceptance attitude towards an adversity, they further contend that: iii) a person cannot be rated on the basis of one of his or her aspects; and iv) the world cannot be rated on the basis of one of its aspects. All these contentions are true and therefore an acceptance attitude is true. • Help the client to see that an acceptance attitude has three non-extreme components: i) an 'aspect evaluation' component which again acknowledges that it is possible and realistic to evaluate a *part* of a person or what has happened to that person; ii) a 'negation of devaluation' component which asserts that the idea that it is not possible to evaluate globally a person or life conditions; and

	Rigid/extreme attitudes	Flexible/non-extreme attitudes
	known as the 'part-whole' error. As such, a devaluation attitude is illogical.	iii) an 'assertion of acceptance' component which holds that the presence or absence of the adversity does not change the fact that: a) the person is fallible, unrateable, complex and everchanging; and b) that life is complex, unrateable and everchanging. Given this, encourage the client to see that that all three of the above components are non-extreme and are logically linked together by being non-extreme. Consequently, an acceptance attitude is logical.
	• Have the client focus on the emotional, behavioural and thinking consequences of their devaluation attitude and encourage them to see that these consequences are unhelpful and unconstructive to them in the long term.	• Have the client focus on the emotional, behavioural and thinking consequences of their acceptance attitude and encourage them to see that these consequences are helpful and constructive to them in the long term.

Suggested further reading

DiGiuseppe, R.A., Doyle, K.A., Dryden, W., & Backx, W. (2014). *A Practitioner's Guide to Rational Emotive Behavior Therapy. 3rd edition.* New York: Oxford University Press.
This is the third edition of a well-received book on REBT. It has a discursive feel to it and will appeal to those who like a broad approach to therapeutic matters. As the title makes clear it is a guide for practitioners and a lengthy one too.

Dryden, W. (2009). *How to Think and Intervene Like an REBT Therapist.* Hove, East Sussex: Routledge.
In this book, I attempt not only to describe a variety of REBT techniques, but I also attempt to capture the clinical thinking that I engage in when deciding on what interventions to make.

Dryden, W. (2012). *Dealing with Emotional Problems Using Rational-Emotive Cognitive Behaviour Therapy: A Practitioner's Guide.* Hove, East Sussex: Routledge.
In this book, I show how a good grasp of the cognitive-behavioural dynamics of the main emotional problems for which clients seek help is crucial to helping them therapeutically.

Dryden, W. (2016). *Attitudes in Rational Emotive Behaviour Therapy: Components, Characteristics and Adversity-related Consequences.* London: Rationality Publications.
This is the book in which I made the case for the usage of the term 'attitude' rather than 'belief' in REBT theory.

Dryden, W., & Ellis, A. (2003). *Albert Ellis Live!* London: Sage.
This book presents and comments on some of the best demonstration sessions of REBT carried out by Albert Ellis that are available. I have included the book here because it shows Ellis' own economical approach to identifying and dealing with people's rigid and extreme beliefs.

References

Beck, A.T. (1976). *Cognitive Therapy and the Emotional Disorders*. New York: International Universities Press.

Burns, D.D. (1980). *Feeling Good: The New Mood Therapy*. New York: Morrow.

DiGiuseppe, R. (1991). Comprehensive cognitive disputing in rational-emotive therapy. In: M. Bernard (Ed.), *Using Rational–Emotive Therapy Effectively*. New York: Plenum.

Dryden, W. (2001). *Reason to Change: A Rational Emotive Behaviour Therapy (REBT) Workbook*. Hove, East Sussex: Brunner-Routledge.

Dryden, W. (2012). *Dealing with Emotional Problems Using Rational-Emotive Cognitive Behaviour Therapy: A Practitioner's Guide*. Hove, East Sussex: Routledge.

Dryden, W. (2015). *Rational Emotive Behaviour Therapy: Distinctive Features. 2nd edition*. Hove, East Sussex: Routledge.

Dryden, W. (2016). *Attitudes in Rational Emotive Behaviour Therapy: Components, Characteristics and Adversity-related Consequences*. London: Rationality Publications.

Dryden, W. (2018). *Flexibility-Based Cognitive Behaviour Therapy*. Abingdon, Oxon: Routledge.

Dryden, W., & Neenan, M. (2004a). *The Rational Emotive Behavioural Approach to Therapeutic Change*. London: Sage.

Dryden, W., & Neenan, M. (2004b). *Counselling Individuals: A Rational Emotive Behavioural Handbook. 4th edition*. London: Whurr.

Dryden, W., & Neenan, M. (2004c). *Rational Emotive Behavioural Counselling in Action. 3rd edition*. London: Sage.

Ellis, A. (1963). Toward a more precise definition of 'emotional' and 'intellectual' insight. *Psychological Reports*, 23, 538–540.

Ellis, A. (1994). *Reason and Emotion in Psychotherapy. Revised and Updated Edition*. New York: Birch Lane Press.

Ellis, A., & Joffe Ellis, D. (2011). *Rational Emotive Behavior Therapy*. Washington, DC: American Psychological Association.

Kellogg, S. (2015). *Transformational Chairwork: Using Psychotherapeutic Dialogues in Clinical Practice*. Lanham, MD: Rowman & Littlefield.

Wegner, D. (1994). *White Bears and Other Unwanted Thoughts: Suppression, Obsession, and the Psychology of Mental Control*. New York: Guilford Press.

Index

For Product Safety Concerns and Information please contact our EU representative GPSR@taylorandfrancis.com
Taylor & Francis Verlag GmbH, Kaufingerstraße 24, 80331 München, Germany

www.ingramcontent.com/pod-product-compliance
Ingram Content Group UK Ltd.
Pitfield, Milton Keynes, MK11 3LW, UK
UKHW020939200926
475569UK00011B/18
* 9 7 8 0 3 6 7 2 7 5 6 3 1 *